The Preschool Curriculum Handbook

The Preschool Curriculum Handbook

by

Roselle P. O'Brien

An Arts-based Curriculum
for Teachers, Directors, Preschools,
and Parents

**The Center for English Language Arts Publishing,
Boston, Massachusetts**

Copyright © 2013

All rights reserved. No part of this publication—except the blank forms provided on pages 107 through 122—may be reproduced, stored in a retrieval system, or transmitted in any form or by any means including electronic, mechanical, photocopying, recording, scanning, or otherwise, without the express written consent and permission of the author.

Publisher website: www.celaonline.com
email for book orders: cela.publishing@gmail.com
subject line: "Orders"
Discount on bulk orders: cela.publishing@gmail.com

Correspondence regarding copyright permissions:
The Center for English Language Arts
P.O. Box 320323
Boston, MA 02132
or email: cela.publishing@gmail.com

ISBN-13: 978-0991050406

**The Center for English Language Arts Publishing,
Boston, Massachusetts**

for Mum

TABLE OF CONTENTS

Introduction

1 The Foundation — 17
What is Learning?
Who Runs the Curriculum?

2 Good Teaching Practices — 21
In a Nutshell

3 Getting Ready — 25
Organizing the Preschool Day
Typical Daily Schedule
Dividing the Work
Joining the Children

4 The Nitty Gritty — 31
Understanding the Fit
Understanding the Grid
Understanding the Squares
Where to Begin: Themes
Where are the Arts?
Arts Areas and Concepts

5 Lesson Planning — 63
Designing the Lessons
Putting it all Together

6 Assessments — 87
What is an Assessment in Preschool?
Report Cards, Rating Scales, and Checklists

7 The Learner with Special Needs — 97
Special Learning Groups and Adapting Curriculum

TABLE OF CONTENTS (cont'd)

8 The Long and Short   **101**

9 Blanks   **105**

    Blank Planning Forms:
    Weekly Grid
    Individual Lesson Plans
    Ordering Supplies
    Teacher Evaluation of Activity
    Student Evaluation of Activity

APPENDIX 1   121
Supporting Documents: The National Association for the Education of Young Children (NAEYC)

APPENDIX 2   141
Supporting Documents: The Massachusetts Department of Early Education and Care (MA DEEC)

APPENDIX 3   149
Supporting Documents: The Massachusetts Department of Elementary and Secondary Education (MA DESE)

BIBLIOGRAPHY   171

Introduction:
Journey and Process

Significant gaps in the education of preschoolers, in the training of their teachers, and in the expectations of how the curriculum frameworks are to be applied in the classroom currently exist in Massachusetts. This work addresses these gaps and provides a bridge.

I have designed an arts-based curriculum for preschool students that applies learning standards and strands from the National Association for the Education of Young Children (NAEYC) guidelines for accreditation, the Common Core State Standards, the Massachusetts Department of Early Education and Care guidelines, and the Massachusetts Curriculum Frameworks in order to support continuity in learning and student readiness for the public schools. It provides preschool teachers with a usable tool and a curriculum upon which they can build their own ideas. It encourages and promotes positive teacher development and improved learning experiences for students.

I arrived at the idea for this handbook as a means of synthesizing current educational standards, guidelines, and regulations regarding preschool education for students aged 2.9 through 4.6 years, and presenting them in a user-friendly package for preschool teachers.

As an educator, I am aware of the shifting trends in educational approaches and policies. The current focus on standardized education and high stakes testing, including the adoption of the Common Core State Standards in Massachusetts and throughout the nation, has brought about significant changes in our approach to education as well as our goals and purpose.

There is a trickle-down from the public schools as they undergo these changes that is reaching and impacting preschool education and preschool learning expectations. As I read and reviewed current documents from NAEYC, the Massachusetts Department of Early Education and Care, the Massachusetts Department of Elementary and Secondary Education, and other agencies, I saw gaps. Many agencies are presenting their goals and guidelines, their standards, their research in support of a particular method for learning, but they appear to be leaving out the essential connection with the preschool teacher. I strongly feel that unless you connect with the preschool teacher and are able to convey what needs to be in a classroom or in a lesson with that person, the learning you seek will not happen.

The current minimum requirements for preschool teacher certification in Massachusetts, as well as in most states, do not include a college degree. The minimum requirements for preschool teacher certification in Massachusetts are a high school diploma or GED, one three-credit course in either Child Growth and Development or Child Psychology, and nine months of work experience. We are taught, as teachers, to support our students in their successes, to present them with learning situations in which they will feel empowered and experience positive growth. We know this yet we do not extend this same awareness to our colleagues. The documents of strands, and standards, learning goals, and guidelines that have been written make many assumptions. They assume that all teachers across the board have had college courses in lesson planning, in curriculum evaluation, in classroom management, in the learner with specialized needs, in curriculum adaptations to support individualized learning, in assessments, in authentic assessments, in creating assessments, in narrative evaluations, in consultation skills, in group and family dynamics. These assumptions are made, the guidelines are written, and there are no bridges for the teachers who may not have had these college courses or who are newly certified and beginning their teaching careers. It is my goal for the handbook I have created to be that bridge.

I began my project with the hope of achieving the following:

- A curriculum and handbook for preschool that aligns with the current learning standards, guidelines, and frameworks

- A curriculum and handbook for preschool that are a usable tool upon which teachers can build their own ideas

- A curriculum and handbook that support continuity in learning and student readiness for entering the public schools

- A curriculum and handbook that provide positive teacher support

- A curriculum and handbook that offer concrete tools for lesson planning, adapting lessons to meet individualized needs of students, and the necessary tools and strategies to authentically assess student growth and learning

The task of designing a curriculum is one of many layers. I felt it was important, when creating my curriculum, curriculum approach, and handbook, to look ahead to the learning expectations of the primary grades, kindergarten through five, and what young preschool learners will experience as they enter and progress through these grades. I explored the curriculum frameworks in the arts, English language arts, mathematics, science, history and social studies, and health. I used this information as a trajectory for my over-arching curriculum goals.

In order for me to meet my curriculum goals, I selected the documents whose learning standards and guidelines I would use as the foundation of my curriculum design. I am a strong supporter of education through the arts and I am an experienced preschool teacher. It was my desire to create a true arts-based curriculum, one that moved beyond the crafts activities that are typical in preschools. I followed the format found in the Massachusetts Arts Curriculum Framework (1999) and selected the arts areas, (music, dance, visual arts, and theater arts,) and the learning standards and strands that would be appropriate for students ages 2.9 through 4.6 years. I did the same, using the Common Core State Standards and the Massachusetts Curriculum Frameworks, for the learning areas of English language arts, mathematics, science, history and social studies, and health.

I incorporated into my curriculum many of the learning goals and learning guidelines set forth by the Massachusetts Department of Early Education and Care and the Massachusetts Department of Elementary and

Secondary Education, including the state regulations for child care centers. I also pulled from the National Association for the Education of Young Children's accreditation standards, position statements, and guidelines for early childhood education. I feel I was successful in synthesizing this information and creating a format for lesson planning that preschool teachers everywhere can utilize.

It became important for me to keep my focus on my stated purpose. Education is a broad area with many significant contributions from teachers around the world. I did not feel it was my purpose, in this project, to present a political statement—something that is very easy to do as we are all highly invested in our field. Saving that for a different project, I worked towards creating an arts-based curriculum and a handbook for all preschool teachers and early childhood professionals.

The limitations I experienced were the time constraints of a typical preschool day. The time constraints of a preschool day in a childcare center are many as there are many specific activities that must be conducted every day. These activities include toileting schedule, morning and afternoon outdoor time, naptime, snack time, lunchtime, and time for free play. Some students are in school for half-days. Other students are in school two or three days per week. Some students habitually arrive late. All of these factors, and more, impact the students and teachers, the teaching, and the preschool day. I feel my curriculum and handbook are highly effective when rising to this challenge.

The only way to successfully juggle these very real factors was to create a curriculum with enough flexibility to absorb the ricochets of the unexpected, embrace the unforeseen, and have learning adapt and continue. The curriculum I have designed allows for original teacher ideas that include adaptations. I have provided a structure and format within which teachers can create independently and meet their individual classroom needs.

My vision of learning is one that provides teachers and children with a solid foundation for success based on respect, joyful experiences, exploration, imagination, creativity, and collaboration. The curriculum and handbook I have designed, and my approach to curriculum and lesson planning, will provide teachers, directors, preschool professionals, and preschools of all kinds with a cohesive program and strong framework for learning that is geared to supporting and enhancing the individual child's strengths, needs, developmental milestones, and unique gifts while preparing students academically, emotionally, and socially for their positive transition and success in the public schools.

Roselle P. O'Brien
Boston, Massachusetts

The Preschool Curriculum Handbook

The Preschool Curriculum Handbook

1 The Foundation

What is Learning?

Learning, in the public schools, is a series of separate, timed boxes: 10:00–10:45 is Math, 10:45–11:20 is Science, 8:00–8:30 AM on Wednesdays is Health.

Learning in a preschool setting—whether it's a large or small group childcare center or a family childcare—involves everything you do with the children for all of the time that they are there. Every moment is a teaching moment. In these preschools, teachers have a special continuity to their days that they can use to create meaningful learning experiences for their students.

The trend today is to standardize education and make every student, teacher, and school in the country accountable for the same content. This approach has students taking high-stakes tests (MCAS in Massachusetts, FCAT in Florida, STAAR in Texas, MSP and HSPE in Washington, to name a few.)

The long-reaching arm of standardized education is now pulling in preschools and preschool learning. Preschool teachers are being held accountable by parents and public schools for curriculum content in English language arts, mathematics, sciences. The high-stakes testing for these very young children are the readiness tests.

But what *is* learning?

Learning is a child's ability to master a task. In preschool, a child's learning tasks include sitting and listening to a story, sharing, realizing that they are indoors and using their indoor voices, choosing to not bite, using words instead of hitting, not putting toys in their mouths, choosing to eat their lunches because noodles in the trash can is not the fastest way to cookies in the mouth, taking turns, and actually resting during rest time.

A child's learning in preschool is recognizing different colors and shapes, pointing to a square and saying, "Square!" Preschool learning includes recognizing the first letter of their names, and gleefully shouting, "R!! That's **my** name!"

How do teachers know what to do when?

Growth and Development

In order to be a preschool teacher, you have to take a course in child growth and development. There are many different lenses you can look through to examine child growth and development. Development in children isn't cut and dried. We can have expectations about when children will walk, when they will talk, when they will succeed at toilet training. But these are ranges. One child may master a developmental task many months before another child masters the same task. Both children have normal development.

Everything hinges on brain development. All the things we do—talking to each other, talking to ourselves, singing, listening, understanding, reading, moving, making plans, thinking, problem solving—are controlled by different and specific areas of the brain. The brain doesn't develop all at once. What does this mean for teachers?

This means that the typical brains of young learners in preschool are not yet able to master abstract thinking, so don't give a child a worksheet until they're in about the third grade. That's when their brains will have developed enough for them to be successful using a worksheet. Third grade is eight years old. We don't want to set children up to fail.

Young learners in preschool, usually ages 2.9 to 4.6 years old, are at a learning stage where they must have things presented to them concretely. They need to hold, and feel, and touch things in order to learn. Curriculum for young learners needs to have lessons that allow the students to touch, and handle, and hold things.

Who Runs the Curriculum?

Curriculum. That's why we're here. You have picked up this book to get insights about curriculum and a solid direction for your lesson plans. There are few things that need to be understood up front:

- The state oversees curriculum. The state oversees and influences curriculum through its regulations for licensure and through its guidelines for preschool learning and preschool learning experiences

- Accreditation agencies, for example, the National Association for the Education of Young Children (NAEYC), oversee and influence curriculum

- These agencies also over-see teacher credentialing and teacher certification, as well as the licensing of childcare centers and family childcares

- Curriculum in public schools is changing across the country. State after state have adopted the Common Core State Standards. Frameworks are being updated to include this different focus for education. The trickle-down is affecting young preschool learners and their teachers

- Preschool teachers are being held accountable by parents and public schools for curriculum content in English language arts, mathematics, and sciences based on the Common Core State Standards and new frameworks

- The Common Core State Standards and the frameworks were not written for the young preschool learner, ages 2.9 to 4.6 years

- High-stakes testing for these very young children are the readiness tests

How do teachers meet the expectations of state agencies, the requirements for accreditation, the desires of parents, the goals of their centers? By following the structure and lesson plans in this book. Copy the forms and use the blank planning forms every week. Use the themes and art concepts. You will be creating your own lessons—lessons that are in step with the Common Core State Standards and the requirements for accreditation—while following a format that will ensure success for your young learners.

It's simple! Read the book, use the forms, apply the themes and art concepts, fill in the blank squares, don't leave any empty—Done!

2 Good Teaching Practices

In a Nutshell

There are forces at work guiding and influencing preschool curriculum: individual states' departments of education and their frameworks, the Common Core State Standards, state regulations for preschools and childcares, early learning agencies (for example, in Massachusetts the MA DEEC) and their publications, accreditation agencies (for example, NAEYC). A large part of creating this handbook has been to make sure my curriculum and curriculum approach meet these guidelines.

What I have done, behind the scenes, is pull from these guidelines, frameworks, and agency publications the learning standards and strands that specifically apply to curriculum. State departments of education and other agencies, such as NAEYC, have long lists of criteria that make for best teaching practices that teachers, preschools, and childcare centers have to meet in order to be licensed and accredited. My purpose here is not preparing preschools for accreditation or licensure. I have selected only the learning standards, strands, and guidelines that direct and support preschool curriculum. This does not include things like how to physically set up a classroom, how far apart cots have to be during naptime, gross motor activities for outdoor play, fine motor activities.

You are the teacher and you will be using this curriculum to create your own lessons. There are many things I don't need to tell you. I know you include gross motor and fine motor activities for your students every day. I know that you know how to arrange your classroom with dramatic play areas and quiet corners. My focus is curriculum. The curriculum I have designed can be used as a template. Take advantage of the themes and art concepts I have listed and included. They already match up with the frameworks. Use your creativity, skills, and knowledge to fill in the Grid with your own lesson ideas—but remember to follow my plan in order to stay in step with agency and school guidelines for learning.

The written curriculum is only one part of teaching. Although we teachers all have different personalities and different approaches to presenting our lessons, there are still common factors as to what makes good teaching. Here are some teacher guidelines in a nutshell (based on NAEYC "All Criteria Document" updated 01/10/2012 and the MA DESE 2003 *Guidelines for Preschool Learning Experiences*.) As you read, think about them, what they mean to you, and what they mean to your students:

- All children are capable of learning

- Families are the primary caregivers and teachers of their young children

- Teachers have to know about child growth and development in order to create, facilitate, and build lessons for their young learners

- It is important for teachers to work together and to work in partnership with families. There need to be open lines for two-way communication.

- It is important for teachers to be knowledgeable about the cultural diversity of their students, their students' families, and the communities within which their students live. This includes knowledge about cultural backgrounds, languages spoken at home, and different family structures.

- It is the teachers' responsibility to foster and create a positive emotional climate in their classrooms that supports the emotional well-being of their students.

- Students need to be able to receive support from teachers for their appropriate expressions of emotions, positive and negative—joy, pleasure, and excitement as well as anger, frustration, and sadness.

- Teachers need to pay attention to how they respond to their students. Teachers should respond to their students based on the students' individual needs (for example, differing abilities, temperaments, activity levels, social development, cognition.)

- Young students learn by doing

- No physical punishment ever! No hitting, no shaking.

- No psychological abuse or coercion.

- Never use threats, insults, or derogatory remarks.

- Never withhold—or threaten to withhold—food as a form of discipline.

- Talk frequently with the children. Listen to them with attention and respect.

- Respond to their questions and requests—answer them with respect.

- Have meaningful and extended conversations with each individual child regularly.

I have been a teacher for almost twenty years. There are two lessons I have learned that, I feel, have helped to make me the best teacher I can be. Lesson number one is from a teacher I worked with at my very first preschool: always speak in your classroom as if the children's parents were in the room—whether they are there or not.

Most of the schools in which I've taught have an open door policy and parents can freely come and go in all the classrooms whenever they choose. There shouldn't be a difference in how teachers speak to the students, no matter who may or may not be in the room.

Lesson number two is simple and significant: always crouch down when you speak with your students so that you are at their eye level.

Power and authority are things we don't think about because we are the teachers. We have the power and the authority in the classroom. We use our words to teach our students. We also teach through nonverbal ways of communication. How we stand and sit, our expressions, the way we move our arms or cross our legs are all ways in which we communicate.

We use our voices and say, "Yes, Johnny, your drawing is very nice. I like it a lot," without turning around or looking down because we're in the middle of a thousand things all the time and Johnny walks away feeling bad. Why? Johnny heard all the things we said nonverbally—through our not turning around, not making eye contact with him—and the positive comments that came out of our mouths didn't matter. The message sent nonverbally was louder than the spoken words.

Take that extra second, crouch down, and look your student in eye every time you talk with each other. It makes a difference.

3 Getting Ready

Organizing the Preschool Day

I know how hectic a preschool day can be. Before we jump into the curriculum and lesson planning, we need to take a good look at how the day is arranged.

The typical day in a preschool center is busy. Teachers need to be organized. The teachers in a classroom need to work together as a team or else everything falls apart. The teachers' day needs to be structured and planned.

I've written out a typical preschool daily schedule that begins opening time of the center and ends at center closing time. You can tweak it as needed so that it accurately represents your preschool class schedule in your center.

All too often the only quiet time during the preschool day is naptime. Naptime is a good time to sit down with paper and pen to try to organize teacher plans. It's too easy for one teacher to feel singled out with always taking the children to the bathroom, or always doing clean up, or never putting up a bulletin board of their own, or rarely running Circle Time. Teachers need to know in advance who is going to do what and it needs to be planned so that things run smoothly and fairly. Teamwork, teamwork, teamwork!

Typical Daily Schedule (hours of child care operation 7AM – 6PM)

7:00—7:20 AM	Open/breakfast *Teachers join students for snack*
7:20—7:30 AM	Clean-up from snack
7:30—8:30 AM	Free Play and Centers
8:30—8:50 AM	Clean-up and bathroom
8:50—9:30 AM	Circle Time
9:30—10:15 AM	Morning Activity and Activity Centers
10:15—10:40 AM	Bathroom, snack *Teachers join students for snack*
10:40—10:55 AM	Get ready to go out
11:00—11:40 AM	Outdoor play
11:40—12:00 PM	Back inside, coats off (wash hands etc., sit to be called for lunch)
12:00—12:30 PM	Lunch *Teachers join students for lunch*
12:30—12:40 PM	Bathroom and onto cots
12:40—2:40 PM	Naptime
2:40—3:00 PM	Bathroom, snack *Teachers join students for snack*
	Get ready to go out
3:00—3:40 PM	Outdoor play
3:40—4:00 PM	Back inside, bathroom, sit for Circle
4:00—4:30 PM	Circle Time
4:30—5:00 PM	Afternoon Activity and Activity Centers
5:00—6:00 PM	Free play and Centers

Dividing the Work

Taking turns is as important for teachers as it is for their students. A daily or weekly schedule can be worked out among teachers to vary assignments and to make sure everyone has an opportunity to assist with the bathroom, prepare for activities, support Circle Time, manage activities, clean up, and prepare meals.

Duties that teachers should alternate include (following the sample preschool schedule provided):

- Morning clean up and bathroom time (after Free Play and before Circle). One teacher takes students to bathroom while the other teacher cleans-up and prepares for Circle Time.

- One teacher facilitates Circle Time while the other teacher prepares the morning Art Activity and the activity Centers.

- Both teachers run the morning Art Activity and activity Centers together

- One teacher takes students to the bathroom following the activities. The other teacher cleans up from activities and sets up snack

- One teacher sets up lunches while the other teacher does bathroom duty when class returns from morning outdoor play

- One teacher sits with students during lunch, modeling appropriate social skills, while the other teacher starts to set up cots for naptime. One teacher takes students to the bathroom while the other helps children settle quietly on their cots to nap/rest.

These are a few example situations where teachers need to plan in advance how they will share and divide classroom duties and responsibilities so that each teacher's skills and talents will be equally supported and will equally contribute to the children's learning.

Make a list of duties. Assign a teacher for each duty. Decide among yourselves whether you want it to be a weekly assignment or to have it change more or less frequently. The actual schedule needs to be something that works for your teachers in your classroom. Some considerations you need to remember when making the schedule are: who works which days; the schedule needs to cover the entire day, mornings and afternoons, opening to closing; ask teachers their preferences beforehand—sometimes one teacher doesn't mind doing certain duties, for example, changing diapers while somebody else would rather sweep the floor every day forever than change diapers—because people like to feel that they are part of the planning.

Joining the Children

Modeling for your students how you want them to behave is vital. Teachers must show their students how to ask for what they want, what kind of voice to use indoors, how to sit in a circle. All the things you want them to do, you have to do for them first.

If you want your students to be able to sit at the table appropriately during snack times and at lunch, you have to show them how to do it. This means teachers have to sit with their students while they are eating, right there at the table. We are adults. We already know how to behave. Our students are very young children who still think biting each other is an effective way to communicate.

Sit at the table. Enjoy that tiny chair and your knees up against your neck. Turn to your left and say with a big smile, "Charlie! What do you have for lunch today?" and wait eagerly for his response. Turn to another student and ask, "Tatiana, what color is the blanket on your bed at home?" Model appropriate table manners. The children will catch on fast. Support and applaud them when they do remember. Say please and thank you all the time. Ask, "Juan, would you like more juice?" or "Rayna, do you remember today's special number?"

Meal times and snack times are opportunities to check-in with the students about Circle Time, to ask them their thoughts about the morning activities—what they liked, what they didn't like—to ask them what things they'd like to learn more about. What you teach, your lessons, need to be guided by your students. Ask your students what they'd like the books you read with them to be about. Listen to their answers.

4 The Nitty Gritty

Understanding the Fit

In order to synthesize things and put everything in a user-friendly package, I first read all the requirements as presented by NAEYC, the Common Core State Standards, state regulations, and the guidelines and frameworks written by the department of education and the Department of Early Education and Care. I took all the information and created an approach to lesson planning—*The Preschool Curriculum Handbook*—that meets all the requirements so that you don't have to worry.

My next step was to translate all of this into a simple format that teachers can use to bump up their lessons and make sure their curriculum meets these standards in education.

This curriculum uses Centers—three Centers—every day at both the morning and the afternoon activity times: (1) the main Arts Activity Center, (2) the Math Center, and (3) the Science Center. There is also a Writing Center but it's used at a different time during the day.

In the morning and again in the afternoon, you will set up three tables. One table will be for the morning Arts Area activity. The second table will be the Math Center. The third table will be the Science Center. Your classroom may have a Science or Math area, but that is not the same thing as the activity center. It is a required that preschool students be given opportunities to make choices. Remember: one of the choices a child can make is to not participate in any or all planned activities. And that's okay!

It is also required that children have time each day for free play and time each day for more structured learning and exploring. Having and using Centers is the best way for providing opportunities for your students to make choices while still presenting and teaching your curriculum lessons and providing structure.

It is key for teachers to understand that things need to be taught in a particular way and that their lesson plans absolutely must contain certain elements. What does this mean in the real world? It means use the blank forms in this book! Make copies and use the lesson plan blanks when you design each lesson you're going to teach. Use the weekly lesson plan grid and make sure you fill in all the squares. Then implement **all** of it! Implement every step and component of each lesson. If you skip some parts, leave other parts out—it's all for nothing.

Understanding the Grid

I call my blank lesson planning form "The Grid" because it looks like a grid. The Grid is a series of squares—of blanks—that you fill in as you brainstorm your lessons. It's really a weekly map for the lessons you're going to plan and teach. Hint: it might be helpful to have a copy of it in front of you while you read this section.

Let's take apart the Grid!

Weekly Planning Grid   Teacher: Classroom: Dates:

	Monday	Tuesday	Wednesday	Thursday	Friday	
THEME:						
Arts Area & Concept	Dance	Visual Arts	Music	Theater Arts		
Literature						
Literacy & Language Building						
Writing Center						
Math Center						
Science Center						
Morning Activity & Critique						
Afternoon Activity & Critique						
Home and Family Connection						
Diversity Connection						
Story Telling: All About Me!						

The Preschool Curriculum Handbook

What do we see?

- Each Grid is for one week of school, Monday through Friday
- There's a place to write the week's theme at the top
- There are four Arts Areas (Dance, Music, Theater Arts, Visual Arts)
- Each Arts Area is given its own day—its own square—and the fifth day is a free choice
- Literacy & Language Building has a square
- Math has a square
- Sciences have a square
- Morning Activity has a square
- Afternoon Activity has a square
- Both the Morning and the Afternoon Activity have a "Critique"
- Home and family connection has a square
- Cultural diversity connection has a square
- Story Telling: All About Me! has a square

The squares of the Grid are blank until you fill them in with your ideas for lessons. Fill in all the squares every day for the week and your lessons will have all the required elements to meet agency guidelines and make your director proud.

Let's take apart the squares!

Understanding the Squares

Each square is an essential element of learning and of the curriculum. None can be skipped or left blank. If any are skipped or left blank, the lessons you teach will not be meeting state requirements, accreditation requirements, or be matching up with the Common Core State Standards or state curriculum frameworks.

Don't be alarmed as you read this section, especially when you get to the Arts Concepts. I know a first reaction can be, "I don't know anything about music!" or "I'm not a dancer! What do I know about dance?" or "Theater Arts! Are you serious? How am I supposed to plan lessons and teach that?" Don't worry. All of that will be explained in section 5: Lesson Planning. Right now we're looking at what type of information gets written into each square. No jumping ahead!

Make a copy of the Grid and have it in front of you while you read. It will be easier than flipping back and forth.

1. **Arts Areas**

    There are four Arts Areas: Dance, Visual Arts, Music, and Theater Arts. In order to make planning easier, I have designated one Arts Area per day of the week and have left Fridays open as a free choice.

2. **Art Concepts**

    Each Arts Area has its own concepts. In the Visual Arts, for example, some Art Concepts are light and shadow, how art tells a story, landscapes, still lifes, portraits, the quality of line, textures, color, patterns, drawing, painting, a studio class, collaborative art, found art, photography, sculpture, film.

    In Music some Art Concepts are beat, melody, notation, fast and slow, high and low, loud and soft, the sound of different instruments, jazz, blues, hip hop, rap. rock and roll, classical, international music, music notation.

In Theater Arts, some Art Concepts are comedy, tragedy, characters, dialogues, monologues, telling stories on stage, TV, movies, plays, the audience.

Art Concepts in Dance include ballet, jazz, tap, authentic movement, modern dance, telling a story through body movement, music and costumes, international dance, folk dancing.

The Art Concept you are focusing on (for the day or for the week or for three weeks—the choice is yours) in the morning and afternoon activity gets written in here.

3. **Literature**

This square is the special book you will read during Circle Time that is about the Theme, the Arts Area, and the Art Concept for the activity you are teaching. You write the book's title and the names of the author and illustrator in the square. Remember: you should be selecting books for the week that are about the week's theme in addition to each day's special book that will be read during Circle Time. All of these books need to be made available for the children to read and explore, with and without teacher support, individually and in small and larger groups. Alternate the books, put some in your classroom's library area, share others at naptime.

4. **Literacy & Language Building: Special Letter for the Day and Special Words for the Day**

This square is the things you are specifically doing to teach reading, writing, and speaking skills. I have included vocabulary word lists in the next chapter for each of the Arts Areas. These vocabulary lists are to help. You can add your own words, too. Pick three or four words that go with your Theme, Arts Area, and Art Concept. Write the words in the square.

On the day you teach that particular lesson, use the vocabulary words you have written down in the square. Teach them during Circle Time. Build on them during the week. When you read the special book, point out while you read and say, "Oh, look! Here's one of our special words for today! It's BANJO. Can everyone say BANJO? It begins with the letter B and what's our special letter for today? That's right! Our special letter for today is B! Good job remembering! What sound does the letter B make? Excellent! That's exactly right! B goes buh..." and continue reading the story.

That's the easiest way for me when I lesson plan, to have a "Special Letter for the Day." It's simple, direct, and absolutely is a significant part of literacy and language building—alphabet letter and sound recognition. It also can be easily worked into many things in the course of the day.

5. **The Writing Center**

    Writing is an important part of literacy. Your students need to be encouraged as writers and given opportunities to write. Two or three times a week add a Writing Center activity to the mornings and afternoons. Give the students another choice! Preschool children are full of stories but unfortunately don't have the writing skills developed yet to enable them to put them on paper. Teachers need to take the time to scribe for their students. A great on-going Writing Center activity would be making a book. Staplers that do saddle stitch—where you fold several sheets of regular sized paper in half and put in three staples down the center at the fold—are easy to come by at any office supply store. It's a quick way to make a blank book for your students to fill with drawings or treasures found on a walk through the neighborhood. Sit down with each student and tell them to share the story of their book with you so that you can write down their words for them. Afterwards, everyone can read each other's stories! The students' books can be read and shared with the class at Circle Time and kept in the classroom's library area where parents can read them, too.

I usually set up the Writing Center during free play times in the morning and again in the afternoon, a minimum of three times a week. Many children like to take a break from other imaginative play and sit down at the table and participate in writing activities. The Writing Center activity is a good focus. You can use books, stories the students have written, drawings to which words and a story can be added. The students can be presented with choices of writing a story (with teacher support and scribing,) or letter copying and writing their name. These can easily be incorporated into a Writing Center activity for your children. Teachers need to provide their students with different and varied opportunities to write.

6. **The Math Center**

It is important to always provide your students with opportunities to write. Make sure you have, at the Math Center a cup of pencils and a stack of paper so that students can write—regardless of what the specific Math Center activities are for the day!

My curriculum uses activity Centers for both the morning and the afternoon activity times. What this means is, in the morning and again in the afternoon, you will set up three tables. One table will be for the morning Arts Area activity. The second table will be the Math Center. The third table will be the Science Center. Your classroom may have a Science or Math area, but that is not the same thing as the activity Center.

The Math activity should be tied to the day's Art Concept. I know this doesn't always work. BUT the Arts Area's "Special Words for the Day" (the art vocabulary) can be worked in. For example, if one of the Special words is "note" (as in musical note,) you could cut out and prepare in advance large-sized musical notes ♪ or ♫. The students can count them using the "Special Number for the Day." Simple addition and subtraction can be included. Or there could be many notes in different colors that the students can sort according to color. Or there could be many notes in varying sizes that the children can sort using terms "small, bigger, biggest." The students could practice writing the numbers after sorting them in different groups.

If the Art Concept for the day is Still Lifes and the students are working with fruit or flowers for the art activity, fruits and flowers could be used in the math activity: counting, matching, sorting, grouping, adding, subtracting, putting in lines, arranging so that a bunch of flowers shape a circle, or square, or triangle.

Language and Literacy topics can be used in the Math Center. If the letter for the day is B, the teacher can create many letter Bs of varying sizes or colors that the children can group into different classifications.

Math: Special Number for the Day

The same way you pick a "Special Letter for the Day," you can pick a "Special Number for the Day." Use the special number all day long. If the day's special number is 4, you can count four carrot sticks or four crackers at snack time. Children can help set the table for snacks by taking four cups at a time to put on the table. Cut a child's sandwich into four sections and have them count with you. Use your imagination!

7. **Science Center**

   It is important to always provide your students with opportunities to write. Make sure you have, at the Science Center a cup of pencils and a stack of paper so that students can write—regardless of what the specific Science Center activities are for the day!

The third table is for the Science Activity Center. It would be wonderful to tie the morning and afternoon science activities in with the day's Art Concept. For example, if the day's Art Area is Music and the Art Concept for the lesson is examining and exploring different instruments in an orchestra (like the violin, the piano, the flute,) you could have the students listen to—and even watch because everything is on youtube including these suggestions and CDs/DVDs are easy to burn—famous musicians play *Flight of the Bumblebees* on different instruments—Yuja Wang plays *Flight of the Bumblebees* on the piano, Itzhak Perlman plays *Flight of the Bumblebees* on the violin, James Galway plays *Flight of the Bumblebees* on the flute—and have the focus be on bumblebees at the Science Activity Center. The students could have books about life cycles of bumblebees, pictures of bumblebees at flowers, examine a beehive, taste honey. Science questions could be: what kind of weather do bumblebees like? Do bumblebees sleep? If bumblebees sleep, do they shut their eyes? How many eyes do bumblebees have? Do bumblebees snore? What if you woke up and a bumblebee was wearing your pajamas? (A question that ties in with Writing Center and literacy activities.)

8. **Morning Activity/Afternoon Activity**

   It is required of preschools in daycare centers that there be a morning activity and an afternoon activity every day, and that these two activities be different. The reason they need to be different is that some children are enrolled for a full day, will be present for both activities, and their learning needs to be ongoing not re-runs.

   Because the Math Center and Science Center activities are more exploratory and tend to have choices within them, these don't have to change so much. Just remember to provide students with those options at each center (e.g. at the Science Center on Bumblebee Day have books and beehives in the morning and pictures of bees in flowers and honey to taste in the afternoon—but the focus stays on bumblebees all day long.)

9. **Home and Family Connection**

   It is absolutely essential for your students' learning to be connected to their homes and to their families and community.

   Research from the U. S. Department of Health and Human Services—the NICHD Study—has shown that "features of the family and of children's experiences in their families proved, in general, to be stronger and more consistent predictors of child development," (NICHD, 2006, 22).

The NICHD study showed, when looking at cognitive and language development outcomes in the children they studied, that "family and parent features were more important predictors of this development..." (NICHD, 2006, 22).

The study also showed that "the quality of the family environment [and] the extent to which family provided cognitively stimulating experiences (such as having books in the home, taking trips to the library, and the like) for the child," were the factors that made the difference (NICHD, 2006, 22).

The NICHD study concluded, from its research, "Many family features are more strongly and more consistently linked to child development outcomes than are child care features for children up to age 4 ½ (and even into kindergarten)," (NICHD, 2006, 25).

What does this mean for you, the teacher? You have to get parents involved! Parents need to be included in the planning and in the teaching of the preschool curriculum. It's a must. How do you do this?

- Monthly classroom newsletter
- Weekly classroom newsletter
- Daily sheets home

PLUS you invite parents and families to give you suggestions of weekly themes and of things they would like to see their children learning about in school. Then you **use the parent suggestions and include them in your lessons**. Choose a parent's suggestion for a weekly them and build lessons around it. Give the parents credit for their ideas—in writing!—on your curriculum sheets and lesson plans, and in the monthly/weekly/daily newsletters and sheets home. Use the Fridays (they don't have a specific Arts Area attached to them) as a day for a parent suggestion activity. It doesn't have to be every Friday. It can be one or two Fridays a month: Parents Curriculum Day. Invite the parents to come in and participate!

Not all parents are able to come in, but all parents have ideas. Tap into them. It's another way of relationship building between teachers and parents while acknowledging the significant role of parents in teaching their children. Bring your students' homes and families into your classroom. They are too important to simply be a bulletin board on the wall.

In this square, write down what you're doing (for the week or as a part of each lesson,) that is a connection to each child's home and family. Some ideas include recommending books to read together at home, songs to sing together at home, if there's an event on the weekend that relates to classroom learning (for example, apple picking during your classroom's All About Autumn Week or special stories read aloud at the library, CDs you can burn with classroom songs that the children can take home to listen to or for a sing-along with parents and families.) Write down if you're using a parent idea or parent suggestion.

10. **Diversity Connection**

Diversity includes gender diversity, cultural diversity, diversity in family structure, age diversity, language diversity, and diversity of ability. The NAEYC "All Criteria Document" clearly explains each of these areas (on pages nine and twenty to twenty-two):

- Gender diversity – may include men and women in nontraditional roles. For example, men and women are equally capable.
- Age diversity – non-stereotypical, older and younger people doing the same jobs and/or a variety of jobs (e.g. not all old people are grandparents), photographs, stories about younger/older siblings
- Language diversity – bilingual labels in the classroom, bilingual communication, multilingual music selections, the use of sign language
- Diversity of abilities – refers to range of ability, including but not limited to disability
- Cultural diversity – conversations, books, posters, and other materials that demonstrate people of various cultures in non-stereotypical ways
- Diversity of family structure – non-stereotypical evidence may include recognition of variations in family structure (ex. photographs of children's families, etc.).

As you plan your curriculum, think about places where differences in your students can be celebrated! Pick at least two Diversity Connections for each day's lesson. I always have one be about how I'm adapting each lesson to meet the individual learning needs of my students.

More Diversity Connection suggestions:
- Adaptations to your lesson that you might need to make to accommodate individual students needs (including the needs of English language learners, students who might have mobility issues, students with disabilities, younger and older students in the same classroom)

- Planning special lunches or snack times where students can bring in different food that they eat at home to share with the group (for example, food from India, food from Ireland, food from Africa). Parents are invited, too! Watch out for allergies.

11. **Storytelling: All About Me!**

    Your students need an opportunity to share—about themselves, their families—and the lessons you teach need to connect with your students' real lives. Here is the square to make that happen.

    Storytelling and sharing can be woven into Circle Time each morning and afternoon. Ask your students questions about who they are, their likes, their dislikes. Encourage your students to share stories that connect their home and family lives to the day's activities or the week's theme.

    If, for example, the theme for the week is All About Animals, have your students, one-by-one, dance (or move) like their favorite animal while the rest of the students try to guess what that favorite animal is. Or have your students, one-by-one, sing like their favorite animal while the rest of the students try to guess what animal it could be singing that song.

    Have your students bring in pictures from home to share stories about themselves, their families, and their communities. Make it personal! Make it real!

12. **What about "The Critique"**

    The Critique is an essential part of the morning and the afternoon Art Activity and will be discussed in detail in section 5 Lesson Planning.

Where to Begin: Themes

Sometimes it can be hard figuring out where to begin when it comes to lesson planning. This curriculum begins with Themes, Art Areas, and Art Concepts.

Let's take apart Themes!

Face it, there are some things you have to teach that **must** be a part of preschool curriculum. These things are guided by state agencies, state regulations, guidelines for learning, state curriculum frameworks, and standards for accreditation. I have found the easiest way to teach these learning areas is to make them weekly Themes.

There are fifty-two weeks in a year and fifty-two weeks in a full-year preschool program. There are thirty-six weeks in a school year program, but there are still fifty-two weeks in a year. Most centers are open year round. Even if your center has a program that runs on a school year calendar, they must offer programming and curriculum for all of the weeks they are open.

Some centers may have one or two week mandatory closing times during the year when everything shuts down and everyone takes vacation. That leaves fifty weeks of curriculum to be planned.

Choose a different theme for each week. During that week, the Art Concepts and the lesson plans will connect with the theme you pick. Themes are overarching. They hover. Themes are the weekly glue that holds everything you teach together.

Here is a list of weekly Themes that cover most of the "must teach" learning areas. Use them. Add to them. Don't leave any out!

Themes that Must be Taught

Math:

- Shapes
- Colors
- Counting 1-10 (including simple adding and subtracting: more than/take away)
- Textures: rough, smooth, hard, soft, dry, wet, cold, hot, bumpy, shiny
- Let's Measure
- All About Money

Science:

- The Weather
- Spring
- Summer
- Fall
- Winter
- Days of the Week
- Months of the Year
- The Seasons
- My Five Senses
- Let's go to the Beach
- Who Lives in the Ocean
- Our Barnyard Animal Friends
- Who Lives in the Trees?
- How do Flowers Grow?
- Dinosaurs
- Sharks
- Why Snowmen Don't go to the Beach (or Why Snowmen Don't Surf)
- What's in the Sky?
- Are Rocks Alive?

- Insects
- Bumblebees and Flowers
- What do Plants Eat?

History and Social Studies:
- Our Town
- Where We Live
- Our School
- Following the Rules
- Our Families (or Meet My Family)
- This is my House (include street, town)
- This is my Classroom
- Helpers in our Neighborhood (police, firemen, librarian, teacher, etc.)
- America (the flag, the national anthem, picture and name of president, words to the Pledge of Allegiance)
- Holidays in the United States: Presidents' Day, Columbus Day, Independence Day, Martin Luther King, Jr. Day, Thanksgiving
- Recycling
- Cleaning up our Community
- Planting a Garden

Health and Safety:
- Healthy Foods
- Brushing my Teeth
- Ouch! (first aid, band aids, don't touch other people's boo-boos)
- Going to the Doctor
- All the Parts of Me (naming parts of the body—arms, legs, feet, hands, head, eyes, etc.)
- Bath Time
- Let's Exercise (or I like to Move my Body!)

- Safe/Not Safe
- What Goes in my Mouth?

Diversity:
- The Languages We Speak
- Friends with Special Needs
- How We Work (different jobs people do including work done at home)
- Come Over to my House!

Multiple Content Areas:
- Let's Cook (include safety measures and hand washing when preparing food)
- Going Shopping Week: Creating a Store! (food shopping, clothes, shoes, pharmacy, toys, music and movies)—set up a store with play money for the children to use.

Literacy and Language:
- Writing my Name
- All About Books
- Going to the Library
- All About Books
- This is a Fairly Tale
- Poems and Rhymes
- Story books about Math topics
- Story books about Science topics

Social-Emotional Development:
- What do you do when you feel this Way?
- Taking Turns
- Good Manners

- Our Feelings
- We Don't Hit

Where are the Arts?

The typical preschool morning and afternoon activities tend to be variations on glue and paint. Students glue and paint different colored paper, toilet paper rolls, paper towel rolls, paper plates, feathers, pom-pom balls, pieces of construction paper, pieces of fabric, letters of the alphabet, numbers, shapes, yarn, pipe cleaners, itty-bitty rocks, teeny-tiny shells, and puffy, rolling googlie-eyes.

Preschoolers drive toy cars through paint, paint with brushes, paint with their fingers, paint with their hands, paint with their feet, paint with small toys, paint with dinosaurs, paint with Barbie and Ken, paint with farm animals, paint with sponges, paint with apples, paint with potatoes. They glue bits onto construction paper, onto cardboard, onto paper plates, onto foil, onto tubes, onto their arms. Then they glue these onto paper with their names on them. Sometimes they glue individually. Other times they glue as a group. Or paint as a group. Or paint then glue in the same activity.

Preschoolers go on nature walks carrying small, brown lunch bags into which they put their nature treasures that they find along the way. The students bring these treasures back into the classroom where they glue the leaves onto paper, or paint with the leaves, or glue the flowers onto paper, or paint with the flowers, or paint with the pinecones, or glue the pinecones onto paper. They glue their acorns, and tiny rocks, and little crumbs from the outdoors onto different colored construction paper. Sometimes things get sprinkled with glitter.

In the spring, students make flowers with pipe cleaners and cut up egg cartons. The students use ribbons and fabric to make Mother's Day sachets. They paint and they glue and they paint and they glue.

Teachers often set up play dough at a table as a choice during free play, announcing, "The Block Area is open, Dramatic Play Area is open, Lego's are open, and there is play dough."

Where are the Arts?

The Arts are right here!

The Arts Areas and Concepts

There are four separate Arts Areas that I focused on in designing this curriculum approach. The four areas are Dance, Music, Theater Arts, and Visual Arts. Each arts area has its own standards, strands, vocabulary, and master artists. Each Arts Area also has its own Art Concepts.

Teaching the arts to young children is often introducing them—sometimes for the first time!—to new and different ideas, sounds, movements, and ways of looking at their world. A preschool teacher, teaching in the Arts Areas, doesn't need to be intimidated or feel that they don't know enough to teach about Dance, or Music, or Visual Arts, or Theater Arts. So much of what we teach our young students is how to look, how to listen, how to begin and explore.

It is absolutely necessary and required, when teaching any of the Arts Areas, to provide for your students examples of the work of famous artists—of masters. The students must be shown the work of famous artists as examples for each and every Art Concept you teach, in all of the Arts Areas. Here are some examples:

- Visual Arts - Van Gogh, Picasso, Dali, Odilon Redon, Georgia O'Keefe, Nir Alon, Gertrude Jekyll, Peter Zumthor, *Toy Story,* Maya Lin

- Music - Ella Fitzgerald, Louis Prima, U2, Eliza Doolittle, Yo Yo Ma

- Theater Arts - My Fair Lady, Oklahoma, Lion King, Peter Pan, Beauty and the Beast, Jim Henson, Julie Taymor, Peter Schumann

- Dance - Baryshnikov, Nureyev, Gene Kelly, Fred and Ginger, Isadora Duncan, Shabba Doo, Michael Flatley, Martha Graham, Robert Joffrey, the Nicholas Brothers.

The computer is my best friend. When I'm planning a lesson and I don't know what to teach and my mind is completely smooth and empty, I do a search on the computer. I always find what I'm looking for—and lots of things I didn't know existed. Nine times out of ten, I suddenly have the perfect idea for a great lesson because of something I stumbled on when using a search engine. Make the computer your best friend.

Now, let's take apart the Arts Areas!

Strands and Standards
Note: The Strands, Standards, and vocabulary words used below in each of the Arts Areas are from the Massachusetts Arts Curriculum Framework and are written out in detail in Appendix 3 at the end of this book.

Picture a learning Strand as an umbrella curving over, protecting, and holding together the different aspects of the art of Dance (or any other of the Arts Areas,) that you will be teaching your students. The different aspects beneath the umbrella are the Standards.

1. **Dance**

    Dance is moving our bodies. Think about the children in your class. It's hard to get them to stop moving their bodies! Perhaps you could think of Dance as controlled wiggling.

Dance is also about how we can communicate with each other through moving our bodies. Movements and gestures—nonverbal communication—are an everyday part of our lives. We wave hello to each other, we nod our heads to mean "yes," we tap our foot to show impatience or annoyance. We frown, we smile, we shake our fists. We glare, we stare, we swoop down and spin as we hug our children. It's amazing how quickly a song with body movements turns into loud chaos and laughter because of how involved the children become in the sheer joy of moving. Look at how much your students love to move, and giggle, and roll across the floor. We're dancing all the time.

The Strand for Dance: Students learn about and use the symbolic language of dance

The Standards for Dance:
- Movement Elements and Dance Skills
- Dance as Expression
- Performance in Dance
- Critical Response
- Interdisciplinary Connections

The Preschool Vocabulary for Dance includes:

balance — a state of bodily equilibrium; the point where the sum of all the forces acting upon the body equals zero and the forces are in equilibrium

flexibility — range of motion determined by a person's particular skeletal structure and muscular elasticity

gesture	the movement of a body part or combination of parts with the emphasis on the expressive aspects of the move
locomotor	implies movement in space including walking, skipping, hopping, galloping, sliding, leaping
nonlocomotor	implies movement in place and includes twisting, movements balancing, and extending
personal space	the "space bubble" or the kinesphere that one occupies; it includes all levels, planes, and directions both near and far from the body's center
shape	the positioning of the body in space: curved, straight, angular, twisted, symmetrical, asymmetrical
space	the medium in which movement takes place; a defined area
tempo	the rate of pulses or beats in music; the relative speed at which a dance phrase or composition is to be performed; pace
unison	dance movement takes place at the same time in a group

Art Concepts

Art Concepts in Dance include ballet, jazz, tap, authentic movement, modern dance, telling a story through body movement, music and costumes, international dance, folk dancing.

2. **Music**

   Music is another way we communicate with each other. Through music we share our feelings, our thoughts, our wants, the vastness of space, the beat of our heart. Songs and music make us laugh, make us cry, make us stop in our tracks to listen, leave us wanting more. The essence of music is a pattern—places of sound and places of silence. Music in preschool is an exploration of sound, pattern, rhythm, mood, and instruments.

   The Strands for Music: Students learn about and use the symbolic language of music; Students learn about the history and criticism of music, its role in the community, and it's links to other disciplines.

   The Standards for Music:
   - Singing
   - Reading and Notation
   - Playing Instruments
   - Improvisation and Composition
   - Critical Response
   - History, Criticism, and Links to Other Disciplines
   - Purposes and Meanings in the Arts
   - Interdisciplinary Connections

The Preschool Vocabulary for Music includes:

beat	the unit of rhythm; rhythmic pulse felt in most music
clef	a symbol written at the beginning of a musical staff to indicate the pitch of the notes
compose	to create original music by organizing sound, usually written down for others to perform
melody	rhythmic arrangement of tones in to express a musical idea
notation	system by which music is written
note	the written expression of a sound in music
rest	the written expression of silence in music
tempo	how fasts or slow, the speed of the beat in music

Art Concepts

In Music, some Art Concepts are beat, melody, notation, fast and slow, high and low, loud and soft, the sound of different instruments, jazz, blues, hip hop, rap. rock and roll, classical, international music, music notation.

3. **Theater Arts**

Children love to role-play. They love to play dress up. They pretend to be firemen, dancers, movie stars, singers, teachers. Theater Arts come naturally to students. They immediately act out all or portions of stories read aloud to them, eagerly chase each other around the classroom pretending to be the gingerbread boy.

The Strands for Theater Arts: Students learn about and use the symbolic language of theater; Students learn about the history and criticism of theater, its role in the community, and it's links to other disciplines

The Standards for Theater Arts:
- Acting
- Directing
- Technical Theater
- Critical Response
- History
- Interdisciplinary Connections

The Preschool Vocabulary for Theater Arts includes:

character	a person, animal, or entity in a story, scene, or play with specific distinguishing physical, mental, and attitudinal attributes
comedy	a drama of light and amusing character, typically with a happy ending
gesture	the movement of a body part or combination of parts, with the emphasis on the expressive aspects of the move
imagery	a term for any expression, reference, or allusion that appeals to the senses, such as colors, sounds, odors, or visual description. Also, the

	collective term for images or a pattern of images in a literary work.
makeup	cosmetics used to change the appearance of the face and other exposed surfaces of the body in order to emphasize characteristics appropriate to a role
performance	the imitation of life in front of at least one other person. In a broad sense, performance refers to the presentation of any kind of entertainment, from play to rock concert, solo presentation to ensemble collaboration
rehearsal	repeated practice in preparation for a public performance
setting	the time and place of a scene or play
sound effects	actual or simulated sounds used to create an aural atmosphere
stage directions	description of direction that indicates actors' movements or stage business, locations on a stage from the actors' position: center stage, stage right, stage left, upstage (toward or at the back of the stage), down stage (toward or at the front of the stage)

stage manager	the head of the production staff who, once the play opens, takes charge of the stage, the actors, and the crews
technical	design and creation of sets lighting, sound, properties, costumes, makeup
tragedy	involve serious action with strong moral implications

Art Concepts

In Theater Arts, some Art Concepts are comedy, tragedy, characters, dialogues, monologues, telling stories on stage, TV, movies, plays, the audience.

4. **Visual Arts**

Exploring the Visual Arts is exploring how we see our world and what it is we're seeing. We communicate through the Visual Arts, through our painting, drawing, film, sculpture, buildings, roads, bridges, photography, fabrics, and furniture. We share who we are. We witness and record our history.

Preschool students need repeated and varied opportunities to touch, hold, create, and explore in order to learn—this is especially true when it comes to the different techniques and media of the Visual Arts. Their Visual Arts experiences need to move beyond the typical gluing and painting activities.

The Strand for Visual Arts: Students learn about and use the symbolic language of the visual arts

The Standards for Visual Arts:
- Methods, Materials, and Techniques
- Elements and Principals of Design
- Observation, Abstraction, Invention, and Expression
- Drafting, Revising, and Exhibiting
- Critical Response
- Interdisciplinary Connections

The Preschool Vocabulary for Visual Arts includes:

collage	a technique to build 2-D images from fragments of printed paper and cloth incorporated into painting
colors – primary	those from which all other colors are derived, cannot be mixed to make: yellow, red, blue
colors – secondary	made from mixing two primary colors together: orange, green, violet
composition	the combination and arrangement of shape, form, color, line, texture, and space so that they seem satisfactory to the artist
foreground, middle	foreground is closest to the viewer; then moving ground, background back; middle ground is in the middle; and background is what appears to be the most distant

media	the materials used in making art (such as clay, wood, stone, paint, paper, wire, feathers, glue, craypas, chalk)
pattern	a decorative arrangement of shapes that repeats in a predictable way
sculpture	any work carried out in three dimensions (for example, statues, relief sculpture). Drawings, painting, flat collage, print making are all usually two-dimensional.
technique	the procedure used in making art such as modeling, carving, etching, painting, filmmaking
texture	the nature of a surface of a painting, sculpture, or building: rough, smooth, patterned, etc. Visual texture refers to the illusion of texture created on a flat surface through line or brush strokes
two-dimensional	physical characteristics of artwork carried out primarily on a flat surface (for example, most drawing, painting, printmaking, photographs)
three-dimensional	physical characteristics of artwork that have depth, width, height, and volume (for example, most sculpture)

Art Concepts

In the Visual Arts, some Art Concepts are light and shadow, how art tells a story, landscapes, still lifes, portraits, the quality of line, textures, color, patterns, drawing, painting, a studio class, collaborative art, found art, photography, sculpture, film, architecture.

5 Lesson Planning

Designing the Lessons

Lesson planning is a weaving of ideas, concepts, and the things you want your students to learn. Learning isn't something that happens only at Circle Time or planned activity times. In preschool, learning happens throughout the day. It's a day of wonderful opportunity—a gift—to have learning be everything you do and share with your students every day that you are together.

Can you hear the birdies singing? See the rainbows in the sky?

Right. Obviously someone isn't considering the reality of trying to lesson plan in a busy center or the reality of life in a preschool day. I know. Believe me, I know. I did call it "hectic" way back on page twenty-five.

Directors tend to want the monthly calendar—in advance—with the themes written in for each week. Then, by the Wednesday or Thursday of the previous week, the director usually will want the teacher's calendar for the upcoming week with the specific lesson plans for each day. How much in advance depends on your preschool. Remember that each lesson will also need materials. Who buys the materials can be different from school to school. Sometimes the teachers get supplies and are reimbursed, sometimes the director gets materials and supplies for each classroom, sometimes there's an art closet for everyone to use. There's also the budget.

The big question: How are you supposed to lesson plan when you can't always get someone to stand with one foot in your doorway for two minutes so you can go the bathroom because everyone is so busy?

The answer: follow the structure for lesson planning that I am sharing with you, use the blank forms I've provided here, and you will create solid lessons that are grounded in the frameworks, in the guidelines for preschool learning, the Common Core State Standards, the regulations, and NAEYC standards.

Let's take a look at the lesson planning form you'll be using!

Lesson Plan   Teacher: Classroom: Date:

Theme:

Art Area/Concept:

Literature:

Responding to Literature:

New Vocabulary:

AM/PM Circle Time:

AM Activity (Arts Area Center):

AM Math Center:

AM Science Center:

AM Writing Center:

PM Activity (Arts Area Center):

PM Math Center:

PM Science Center:

PM Writing Center:

Materials:

This lesson plan form is to be used in two ways:

1. <u>The Shorter Version</u>: when completed is precisely one-page long (one form per lesson.) It is a summing up of **each lesson** you'll be teaching for the week. You hand these in to your director in advance, at the same time you hand in your weekly calendar.

2. <u>The Longer Version</u>: a longer, more detailed version—using the same lesson planning format—of the shorter version. This longer version is written and completed with all the details for **each lesson** you are going to teach.

   Note: In some classrooms there is a morning teacher and an afternoon teacher, and each one does their own lessons and lesson planning. If your preschool is set up this way, then each teacher will complete their own forms. There will be one Lesson Plan form with the morning activities done by the morning teacher and one Lesson Plan form with the afternoon activities done by the afternoon teacher for each day. A blank Lesson Plan form is available in section 9 Blanks. In the following examples I am using the Lesson Plan form you would use if you were the only teacher creating lessons for both the morning and the afternoon activities.

Lesson planning involves paperwork, documentation, and record keeping. There's no way around it. All teachers need to have, keep, and maintain documentation to support every single lesson they teach. I have provided you with two forms: The Grid and the Lesson Plan. They are visual and cognitive aids for you to use when planning your lessons.

The Grid has all the elements you need to include and teach for each of your lessons for an entire week. It's a place for the quick notation, not for the longer details. The Lesson Plan is the place to organize and write all the details of what you are going to teach and how you are going to teach it. The Grid is a place for brainstorming ideas. The Lesson Plan is your script.

Let's break down lesson planning into steps:

When you sit down to lesson plan, you need to have with you a copy of the blank Grid, a copy of the blank Lesson Plan, and a stack of blank paper (or a notebook).

Lesson planning is a two-step process:

Step One: Filling in the Grid

First, you fill in that weekly Grid. Yes, the Grid gets filled in BEFORE you plan the step-by-step of the lessons. As you fill in the Grid, you will definitely be having wonderful ideas about the daily lessons. You should have your blank paper ready to write down your ideas so that you'll have them to use to complete the Lesson Plan. I think it will help if I share with you all my reasoning and thinking as I plan a sample lesson.

Example:

The third week of September is going to be Apple Week in my classroom. I have decided that we will learn about Johnny Appleseed, where apples come from and how they grow on a tree, what an orchard is, how you pick them different kind of apples that people grow and eat, different foods that are made of apples, different parts of the USA and different parts of the world where apples grow and do not grow.

I love music. I usually start planning the Music lessons first because it's easiest for me. I save the harder ones for last. I'll wonder and think about apples and music (hmmmm...anything appropriate for preschool by Fiona Apple? Probably not.) I'll do a search on the computer, (for example, Google, or Dogpile, or Ask, or Youtube.) I'll type in "apple" and "apple music" (realizing as I type that The Beatles will show up a lot because of Apple Records.) Then I'll search again, typing in "songs about apples" because I got a lot of information and links I didn't need about Apple computers and itunes. Ah-ha! I have found that there are actual websites that teachers have put online for the universe to use with preschool songs about apples! There's a song that's sung to the tune of *Yankee Doodle Dandy*, another one sung to the tune of *Five Little Monkeys*. See—not too much looking involved.

But how do you work in Art Themes, and Art Areas, and Art Concepts?

Okay. Let's look at the Grid:

1. Write across the squares, in big letters, at the top where it says "Theme, "—"Apple Week."

2. Monday the Art Area is Dance. What Art Concept about Dance do you want to teach? I don't know about you, but immediately my mind is a blank. What to do? Flip back to section 4 Art Areas and Concepts of this book and look at some the Art Concepts for Dance. Pick one. Sometimes simply reading through them can give you ideas. Or you can read over the learning Strands and the different Standards for Dance. These are the things you need to be teaching and they are also Art Concepts. Ideas may explode!

Let's say you've decided that Monday of Apple Week, the Art Concept for Dance that you will teach is Folk Dances. Why did I pick Folk Dances?

First, I was rather mindlessly searching "apple dances" on the computer. I read something on the list of links that popped up about an African-American dance craze in the early 1900s called The Big Apple Dance. I then went and did a search on a website that has zillions of videos and video clips you can watch, and typed in, "big apple dance." (I didn't know anything about The Big Apple Dance until I read it on the computer search.) The site search resulted in a bunch of video clips on The Big Apple Dance and one gave a lot of background information as well as showing actual people doing the dance. I watched the video clip and thought it would be so much fun to teach it to the kids!

So, if you do these simple computer searches and type in "Big Apple Dance," you'll find all the same information that I did, telling about a dance craze that began in the U.S. in 1937 called the Big Apple Dance. It was a dance started by African-Americans in New Jersey that took off during the Depression, (although it actually is a little older,) just prior to the start of World War II. There are other clips that show you how to do the Big Apple Dance, step-by-step.

There's your Art Concept for Monday Dance during Apple Week. Write it in the square on the Grid: "Folk Dancing" as the Art Concept in the same square as "Dance." But we're not done.

During morning Circle Time, you will be talking with your students about Folk Dances—maybe even have a book about Folk Dances from the United States and other countries. Lots of times I do a quick search on the computer for immediate information that sparks good classroom ideas. For example, there are some websites that give brief and understandable definitions of things (one especially that every single middle school, high school, and college tells their students they cannot site as a source on their papers because anyone can type in and alter the information presented on this website so it's not reliable.)

But I use it all the time. It gives me ideas for lessons. I make sure I double-check the facts other places.

I typed in "folk dance" and got helpful information about what makes a Folk Dance a Folk Dance. Lots of stuff. I got ideas for things I could include in my teaching, information I quickly and easily double-checked on other websites to make sure it was correct before I included it in my lesson plan. Usually, this information gives you a good place to start your talk with the students during Circle Time. The students can ask you questions.

Idea: You can ask the students to take turns, saying if they were going to make up a Folk Dance what would it be like—to explain it first in words and then dance the dance for you and their classmates. Then you could talk with them about a Folk Dance called the Big Apple Dance, tell them what the dance is about, and show them a Folk Dance called the Big Apple Dance.

This should be starting to sound familiar. Yes! Section 4 The Nitty-Gritty! Understanding the Squares!

One more thing. These same websites that have zillions of videos and video clips that you can search through and watch also have instructions for how to save the videos and video clips onto CDs, DVDs, and flash drives. You simply have to type in a search on the website asking how to do it and the video clip explaining all will magically appear. (There are also free downloads available for software that will convert a video to an mp3.) Think about Apple Week. If you work in a preschool that frowns heavily on watching videos, you could put the flash or the DVD into the computer, minimize it so there's no picture, and have only the music playing.

Then on Music day—Wednesday—you could use some of the music the children danced to on Monday as part of the Music lesson, connecting your all lessons.

But what about the Afternoon Activity?

That's right. You do need a second activity for the afternoon. The Big Apple Dance was a huge hit with the children in the morning and they loved it. What to do?

You make the focus of the afternoon Art Activity—the Art Concept—not be Folk Dances. Instead, you make the afternoon Art Concept for Dance be Telling a Story Through Body Movement. (Remember, the morning Art Activity had the Art Concept of Folk Dances.)

During Circle Time, you could ask the children questions about telling a story through body movement, for example, "If I moved my arms like this," (and flap them like a chicken,) what kind of story do you think I might be telling?" The students can shout out, "About a chicken! Or a chicken story!" You could do two or three body movements involving all of your body and/or different parts, you could make faces (laughing, crying) and ask the students what kind of story you're telling with your face. Then you could ask them what kind of story, if apples were alive, would apples tell and what kind of movements would they use to tell their story. Then you could show them the Big Apple Dance.

Aren't you teaching the same Art Activity twice? Yes and no. The focus of each Art Activity and the Art Concept are different. In the morning, you're exploring Folk Dances and in the afternoon you're exploring Telling a Story through Body Movements. The Big Apple

Dance is only a small part of each lesson. The lessons themselves are not the same at all. You'll even be using two different books during morning Circle Time and afternoon Circle Time because the lessons are about two different topics. The literature you choose needs to reflect this.

In the Art Concept square on the Grid you'll have to write in two concepts, an AM concept and a PM concept.

3. In the "Literature" square you'll write in two books titles: a book for Morning Circle Time about Folk Dances and a second book for Afternoon Circle Time about Telling a Story Through Body Movement..

Let's go through the rest of the squares.

4. In the Math Center square of the Grid, write in what you're going to have the children do at the Math Center. Write in the Special Number for the Day, if you choose to use one. (I think you should.) Example: write in the number 2 and put a circle around it to show it's the day's Special Number. Go back to section 4 Understanding the Squares for ideas about what activities to have available at the morning and afternoon Math Centers.

5. Do the same thing for the morning and afternoon Science Centers as you did for the Math Centers—pick Science activities!

6. Home and Family Connections can be made in your lesson planning by incorporating different family information about your students into the lessons.

For example, you know your students' ethnic backgrounds, where they and/or their families may be from originally. You can use this information in your teaching. When teaching about Folk Dances, you could talk about a Folk Dance that's from a country that one of your students or their family are from. Sometimes children take lessons and learn their Folk Dances. They could share these dances with the class.

7. I always remember to include under "Diversity Connection" how I've adapted my curriculum and teaching to accommodate the individualized needs of special learners in my class.

8. In the "All About Me!" square, write down how you are including opportunities for your students to share about themselves. Remember, all the lessons you teach need to be real for the students and connect with their lives. They also need to be given opportunities to share their personal stories and their lives with you and their classmates.

Circle Time is a good place for this sharing to happen. Other good times can be in smaller groups when teachers are reading to students. The students can be prompted to share stories about themselves—especially when they can also connect with the Art Concept for the day or an Art Activity.

Now that the Grid is all filled in, we can move on.

Step Two: Filling in the Lesson Plan Form

You need to complete the Lesson Plan form two ways: the Short Version (that you will hand in to your director) and the Long Version (that you keep as your own script.) Make extra copies of the blank Lesson Plan form. The Lesson Plan form will have some repeat information that you already have written on the Grid.

The Short Version:

- Fill in your name, classroom, and the date. The date you write down is the date the lesson will be taught.

- Fill in the Theme for the lesson. If there are two Themes, write in both

- Write in the Art Areas and Art Concepts (from what you have written on the Grid.)

- Write in for "Literature" the title, author, and illustrator of the book or books you will be reading during morning Circle Time and afternoon Circle Time

- "Responding to Literature" is where you write down how the Arts Activity and the Writing, Math, or Science Center activities connect with the book you read during Circle Time, and how your students are able to respond to the book you shared through these activities. Ideally, you want your students to take the information—the story you have shared with them—and create something new!

  Some examples of "Responding to Literature" are (1) after reading a book about circles with your students they can draw objects that are circular and that are round during their Visual Arts activity about Still Lifes (fruits, various small balls, marbles, etc.; (2) after reading two books—*Black on White* by Tana Hoban and *White on Black*, also by Tana Hoban—the students are given materials that are black and white to create costumes for Dance; (3) you bring to the students' attention during an Art Activity about Music (perhaps with the Art Concept of Music Notation) that the way we write music down—the musical notes—are black written on white paper.

- New Vocabulary is where you write the new vocabulary words about the Art Area and Art Concept you'll be teaching that day.

- AM/PM Circle Time is a quick jotting down of what you're going to do during the Circle Times. Example: AM & PM sing hello song, review the weather, days of the week, Special Number. Introduce three new vocabulary words. Introduce new book by activating prior knowledge about colors (ask students their favorite colors, how colors help you see shapes, what would the world look like if everything was all one color.) Read the two Tana Hoban books.

Remember: Always introduce every book you are going to share with your students by activating their prior knowledge. Get them on the right track and thinking about the theme of the story. (For example, if the lesson is about sharing you could pass out two special stickers to the students but then find there aren't enough to go around—which you already knew because you planned it that way. Wait to see if a student will volunteer to share one of their two stickers. If not, volunteer to share one of your stickers and talk with the class how nice it is to share and that you have a book you're going to read to them that's about sharing.

- Briefly write down the AM Art Activity and Critique

- Briefly write down the AM Math Center activities

- Briefly write down the AM Science Center activities

- Briefly write down the AM Writing Center activities

- Briefly write down the PM Art Activity and Critique

- Briefly write down the PM Math Center activities

- Briefly write down the PM Science Center activities

- Briefly write down the PM Writing Center activities

- Fill in the materials you will need to do your activities for this lesson only

The Long Version:

The long version is not much different than the Short Version. It is in the Long Version where you include all the details of the lesson you plan to teach and how you're going to teach the lesson to the students. There are certain lesson planning forms that include things like "goals," and "purpose," and "objectives." Learning in the elementary grades (and higher) is different than learning in preschool.

In the elementary grades, the goals of lessons that teachers write tend to look similar to this sample of a Grade 4 lesson for multiplication:

> *By the end of the lesson, students will be able to multiply by single digits 2, 3, and 4 with a minimum of 80% success. The students will develop a meaningful understanding of the basic mathematical vocabulary and concepts of multiplication through problem solving.*

In this elementary level lesson plan, there are specific learning objectives—be able to multiply by 2, 3, and 4 with 80% success, understand the basic vocabulary, and understand basic multiplication concepts. There is a specific route through which the learning will take place—problem solving. There is a timeframe within which the learning will happen—by the end of the lesson.

This is not learning in a preschool. Learning in a preschool is about discovery and exploration. There is no "by the end of the lesson," because learning is everything you do for the whole time the child is in the preschool. It's open-ended which means there's no right way or wrong way. There's no "with 80% success." It's always 100% success! Learning goals do exist in preschool but they're thought about, written down, and presented differently.

Putting it all Together

On the following pages, I have written a sample Lesson Plan—Long Version.

Let's pretend that it's Fairy Tale Week!

Lesson Plan

Teacher: YOU!   **Classroom:** Preschool 2   **Date:** Wednesday

Theme: Fairy Tale Week

Art Area/Concept: Music/Singing

Literature: AM: Walt Disney's Cinderella, by Cynthia Rylant, Illus. by Mary Blair

PM: Glass Slipper, Gold Sandal: A Worldwide Cinderella, by Paul Fleischman, Illus. by Julie Paschkis

Responding to Literature: The students will be able to respond to the literature through the Writing Center activities, both AM and PM, which include being given blank books to write (with teacher support) and illustrate their own Cinderella story.

New Vocabulary: beat, tempo

AM Circle Time: hello song, weather, calendar (days, month, season). Special # is 4. Special words: beat, tempo (what they mean). Review of Monday & Tuesday's Cinderella stories—same/different, what they remember/what they don't. Will introduce today's book, Walt Disney's Cinderella, by Cynthia Rylant and illustrated by Mary Blair. I will begin by asking the class, "Has anyone heard the story of Cinderella?" and wait for student responses to generate a brief discussion about Cinderella. I will continue, "Well, today we're going to read Walt Disney's Cinderella," holding up book so everyone can see. "It is written by Cynthia Rylant and illustrated by Mary Blair. Does anyone know what the word illustrated means? Yes, that's right! It's the pictures! Very good answer! The pictures in books are also called illustrations and the person who made the pictures is called the illustrator. I think we first heard that word a few weeks ago. Can everyone said illustrator out loud? Let's say it together—illustrator. Very good! We learned that the pictures in a book—the illustrations—sometimes help tell the story. So, today while I read <u>Walt Disney's Cinderella</u> with you, I want you to look at the pictures and see if you think they help to tell the story." I'll begin reading the story.

AM Activity (Arts Area Center): The students will be taught and will sing as a group the song, "Bibbidie-Bobbidie-Boo" from Disney's *Cinderella* (the movie). They will explore tempo and beat by singing the song faster and slower (tempo) and by clapping along (beat). Critique.

AM Writing Center: Pencils, blank books (saddle stitched in advance,) crayons, markers for children to write and illustrate their own Cinderella story; alphabet letters/cards (can be magnet letters used on a white magnet board, felt with a felt board, playing cards made into alphabet cards that students can use on the table) so that with teacher support students can practice "writing" words, their names, Cinderella, etc. Conversations can be about letter sounds, "What letter sounds like fffff—**f**airy tale--fffff?" and see if the students can pick out F.
[Highlight the letter sounds for the week each day to remind students of their learning and to build on their learning.]

AM Science Center: Fairy Tale Science: Cinderella – (1)Turning Mice into Horses. Pictures of mice will be compared to pictures of horses (similarities/differences, bigger/smaller, etc.) Science question for discussion: can mice really turn into horses? Pictures of mice families and horse families (parents and offspring) will be compared. (2) pencils and blank paper (3) books about baby animals for students to read.

AM Math Center: (at Free Play) Large and small letter "C's" in different colors for the students to classify according to color; letter C's can also be grouped according to size; blank paper and pencils; number cards (with numbers 1-5)—or number magnets and white boards or numbers made out of felt and felt boards—for the students to practice number recognition and to put in numerical order. If you put out multiples of each number, the students can match and group them, by same number, as well; counting bears as manipulatives for students to do basic math (for example, basic addition and subtraction,) and counting using one-to-one correspondance

PM Circle Time: hello song, weather, calendar (days, month, season). Special #4. Special words: beat, tempo (what they mean). Review of Monday & Tuesday's Cinderella stories—same/different, what they remember/what they don't. Will introduce today's book, <u>Glass Slipper, Gold Sandal</u>, by first talking about how pictures tell a story because this book has beautiful and striking illustrations. I'll say to the class, "Does anyone remember what the word illustration means? No? Well, illustrations are the pictures in a story. Remember we learned that word a while back? Can everyone say 'illustrations'? Good! The pictures in a book—the illustrations—sometimes help tell the story. Remember how we learned about Cinderella and read the Disney Cinderella story? That's right! Evie said she had the Cinderella movie at home! Well, today's book is a Cinderella story, too. But it's a different Cinderella story. This Cinderella story is about Cinderella's from many different countries, all over the world. It is a Cinderella story from Korea, from Iraq, from Mexico ---"

[It's an added bonus if you have a student from different countries in your class that are used in the book. This can be talked about, too.] I'll begin reading and pointing out the beautiful illustrations.

PM Activity (Arts Area Center): The students will be taught and will sing as a group the song, "Oh, Sing Sweet Nightingale" from Disney's *Cinderella.* They will explore tempo and beat by singing the song faster and slower for tempo, and by clapping along for beat. The students will then listen to the song, "Oh, Sing Sweet Nightingale," sung in different languages from around the world (German, Dutch, Swedish, French, Hebrew, Spanish, etc.) The students will try to guess the different languages being sung and then try to sing the song in that language. Critique.

[Definitely make sure some of the languages reflect the home languages of your students!]

PM Math Center: (at Free Play) Large and small letter "C's" in different colors for the students to classify according to color; letter C's can also be grouped according to size; blank paper and pencils; number cards (with numbers 1-5)—or number magnets and white boards or numbers made out of felt and felt boards—for the students to practice number recognition and to put in numerical order. If you put out multiples of each number, the students can match and group them, by same number, as well; counting bears as manipulatives for students to do basic math (for example, basic addition and subtraction,) and counting using one-to-one correspondence

PM Science Center: Fairy Tale Science: Cinderella – (1) Glass Slippers Made by Fairy Godmother. Science questions for discussion: Are glass slippers really made by fairy godmothers? How do you really make glass and make things out of glass? Have a pan (or bowl, or tray, or sensory table) of sand and a pan (or bowl, or tray, or sensory table) of baking soda ready for the students to touch and feel as you talk about glass because glass is made out of sand and bicarbonate of soda, which is baking soda; (2) Books: A Day in the Life of a Colonial Glassblower, by J.L. Branse and Fire into Ice: Adventures in Glass Making, by James Houston. Share the pictures and read the books and highlights of the books to the students; (3) Pencils and blank paper

PM Writing Center: Pencils, blank books (saddle stitched in advance,) crayons, markers for children to write and illustrate their own Cinderella story; alphabet letters/cards (can be magnet letters used on a white magnet board, felt with a felt board, playing cards made into alphabet cards that students can use on the table) so that with teacher support students can practice "writing" words, their names, Cinderella, etc. Conversations can be about letter sounds, "What letter sounds like ffffff—fairy tale--fffff?" and see if the students can pick out F.
[Highlight the letter sounds for the week each day to remind students of their learning and to build on their learning.]

Materials: CD of songs (can be burned from one of those websites that have zillions of videos and video clips); sand; baking soda; books

Yes, I can hear you, "Finally—tell us! What is the Critique?"

The Critique

The learning standards and guidelines of the Curriculum Frameworks as well as the guidelines and program standards for preschool and preschool learning want students to be able to:

- "Communicate and defend ideas," (MA English Language Arts Curriculum Framework, 2011, 7)

- "Justify their conclusions, communicate them to others, and respond to the arguments of others...state the meaning of the symbols they choose," (MA Mathematics Curriculum Framework, 2011, 15-16)

- "Participate actively in discussions, listen to the ideas of others, and ask and answer relevant questions," (Guidelines for Preschool Learning, 2003, 7)

The foundation for the skills that students will use and build upon as they move through elementary school into middle school and high school need to be taught starting in preschool. The learning begins now.

How are preschool students supposed to begin learning these skills?

Answer: through the Critique.

The Critique, in a studio art class, is when an artist puts his or her artwork on display for the class. The artist presents the work to the class as a group, talks about what the artwork means to him or her, what it's about, why the subject was chosen, what materials were used to create the piece, why those particular materials were selected and used. The artist thinks about, reflects on, shares the different influences, their thought processes, and the techniques that came together in the creation of this particular piece of art.

The other students in the class then take turns talking about the artwork: things about it they like, things they might question, questions they may have for the artist. They discuss ideas they may have that the artist might want to use and incorporate into the piece, things they see that the artist might not, things the artist could do differently. One by one, the students in the class share their insights with the artist, talk about how they understand, experience, and interpret the artwork.

The Critique experience provides students with an opportunity to present something that they have created. It is an opportunity for students to stand proudly and say, "I made this," and to share what it is that they have created and what means to them with others. The critique is an opportunity for students to give each other positive support, to share their ideas and their thinking, to work together.

And once again it is back to the reality of the preschool classroom. The Critique must happen every day. It cannot be skipped. It doesn't have to be immediately following the Art Activity, especially if artwork isn't ready to be put up and displayed for the Critique. It can happen during Circle Time. It can be during a transition time. Not every single student has to have a turn every single time, as long as every student gets at least two turns per week to present their artwork to the class.

It is important that the "do's" and the "do not ever do's" of behavior, when it comes to the Critique, be explained to the students in advance and reinforced frequently. Teachers need to model appropriate Critique behaviors for their students, showing and teaching appropriate comments to make and questions to ask. Through teacher modeling, students learn how to look at art, how to think about and interpret what they are seeing, and how to include the viewpoints of others in their thinking and understanding.

It doesn't stop there. The elements of the critique translate and carry over from how a student looks at, experiences, and understands art into how a student sees, experiences, and understands life, their place in their lives, and their place in the world.

Critique Do's:

- Say positive things about your classmates' artwork (or say two things you like about the artwork and why you like those two things)
- Think before you speak
- Take turns sharing
- Let the other person finish what they're saying before you begin
- Listen to what other people say

Critique Do Not Ever Do's:

- Don't ever say, "That's stupid," or "I don't like that."
- Don't ever laugh at someone else or at their work
- Don't say mean things
- Don't hurt other people's feelings

Today your students are in preschool. In the flash of an eye, they'll be in elementary school then taking standardized tests—like the MCAS here in Massachusetts. These standardized tests have the expectation that students will be able to think and process information in a particular way. We need to start now—in preschool—teaching children to think critically as well as creatively, to have them stop and consider, to problem solve.

The Critique provides an opportunity to lay this foundation. It is an amazing and positive experience to be able to stand in front of a group and not only say, "I made this," but also to share what it means to you to have made it and why, to own your creativity, and have others witness and support you and your work.

How the Critique Looks in the Classroom

I usually have the students sit on their carpet squares in a circle facing the artwork being displayed, with the student who is presenting standing up next to their artwork. It is important to review the Critique and its process before you begin.

- First, I tell the students that we are going have the Critique and that "the Critique" is the time we share and talk with each other about the art we have made.

- I remind the students that we will be talking about the artwork that's in front of them and not some other piece from a different day.

- I remind the students that they are each going to say two things they like about the artwork and also to ask one question about the art work.

- I remind the artist whose work is being displayed, that they are going to talk with the class about their work. They can talk about what it's called, what it is about, what it represents, what media—what materials—they used to make it and why. They can talk about how it tells a story, where they got their ideas. They can talk about the colors or the texture, what they liked about making it, what was hard to do, what was easy to do.

The number of different students who get to ask questions depends on how the group discussion goes, and that changes every time. It is extremely important for the teacher to keep track of who has presented their art and how many times, who asks a lot of questions, who needs support figuring out questions to ask, and to make the Critique a success. The children in my class really enjoy the Critique!

You can't skip it. Don't leave it out.

6 Assessments

What is an Assessment in Preschool?

Every childcare center and preschool have their own type of assessments that the teachers complete regularly to document student development. Many schools use booklets that they buy already printed and ready to use. These booklets have teachers document student development in areas such as gross motor skills, fine motor skills, social and emotional development, and cognitive development. Sometimes they have pictures of blocks, or teddy bears, or A-B-C letter cubes on the covers.

But what is an assessment? Why do we do them? What are they for?

Assessments in preschool are a two-step process. Step one: they are a process of collecting information about students and about students' work in school. Step two: the information is used to help teachers, parents, and programs make the best possible decisions to support student learning, student development, and the curriculum.

The states, through their regulations, inform teachers, schools, and centers about how frequently assessments are to be made. It is up to each school and each center to select the valid and reliable tests that they are going to use. I believe that assessments of preschool students need to be meaningful and authentic.

Authentic assessments are ones where students are given real tasks to do, (a multiple choice test, for example, is not authentic because students are picking a "right" answer from a given list, which is a total set up,) in order to measure the student's ability to apply and use the new knowledge they have learned. In an authentic assessment, the students are given an open-ended problem. That means there is no "right" answer. Through their process of problem solving, the students are given an opportunity to think about and apply new concepts they have learned, and to continue their learning as they respond to the situation presented. Teachers are then able to assess how well a student can use and apply new learning so that it is meaningful to them—not simply whether or not they got a "right" answer. The true test of a student learning and mastering a task is for that student to be able to take the information they have been taught (about rocks, about stars, about letters in the alphabet, about music, about using their words and not hitting, about a photograph, about ballet, about saying please,) and use it to create something new!

Authentic assessments give students that opportunity, to show their learning through creating something new. Through an activity—through the doing of an activity—the students can show you all they have learned. Given open-ended opportunities, they will surprise you. There have been many times I have watched my students, busy in my mind with doing an assessment in one area, and been completely floored when Karla, as usual, raised her hand to hit Simon—and then stopped mid swing, instead shouting, "That wasn't nice! Give me my paintbrush!" That is an example of learning and of a student mastering a task: not hitting, using her words, making a better choice, applying a lesson in an authentic and real-life situation.

Students need to be assessed during the school day while they are involved in their daily activities, which is more than only during a planned activity time. Students need to be observed and assessed during free play, during meal times, over the course of the day. Observation is key. Teachers need to pay attention.

Report Cards, Rating Scales, and Checklists

Students need to be assessed using different teacher rating systems and approaches. There are three we're going to look at here: report cards, rating scales, checklists.

1. **Report Cards**

   The type of report card, or standardized assessment tool, that you will use for your students is the one provided by your school or center.

2. **Rating Scales**

   Rating scales are a wonderful way of recording information. They are used for student behaviors that aren't easily measured through other types of assessments. Rating scales can be created to meet the assessment needs of any curriculum or program. Teachers can create specific rating scales to meet their individual student's, whole classroom, and learning assessment needs.

   For example, you could create a rating scale for how individual students interact with each other during activities, or during naptime, or during lunch and snack. Another rating scale could focus on students' social skills during activities or during the Critique. The information on these sheets can be shared and communicated with parents. You can review and use the information from these sheets, especially over time, to better understand and support your students' learning and developmental needs.

   It is important, when creating rating scales, that you remember to make sure that the things you write down that you are observing are clear, specific, and things you actually can observe.

The words that you choose to describe the measurement points are hugely significant. Stay away from words such as, "fair" or "good" or "poor" because they are too vague and too subjective. If you use the words "always, sometimes, rarely, never," on your rating scale, (as I have in my examples,) make sure you also have specific, measurable definitions about the frequency of a behavior—how much is rarely? how much is sometimes?—that are the same for each different rating scale. I always note across the top of my curriculum book (for my eyes only but information I will share with parents if they ask,) "Sometimes = 75% or 3 times out of 4 in a week. Rarely = 25% or 1 time out of 4 in a week." How you measure and what your words of measurement mean must absolutely be consistent and unchanging every single time they are applied.

Leave some space at the bottom to include anecdotal information for each student.

You **must** write in a comment in the comment section every time you do a rating scale assessment and for every student. The words you write down as comments are the glue that connect and fully develop the student information you have rated on the assessment. You want to present as full and complete a picture of each student and their development as possible.

Remember: Rating scales are used to assess behaviors.

Student Name_____ Classroom_____

Teacher_____Date_____

Social Skills During Activities

Activity:

_____
_____
_____

Key:

4 – always   3 – sometimes   2 - rarely   1 - never

1. Used quiet/indoor voice   _____

2. Listened to directions   _____

3. Was able to follow directions   _____

4. Took turns with classmates   _____

5. Allowed one person to speak at a time   _____

6. Listened to other people's ideas   _____

Comments: _____
_____
_____
_____
_____

Student Name_____Classroom_____

Teacher_____Date_____

Language Development

Key:

4 – always   3 – sometimes   2 - rarely   1 – never

1. Responds to questions from teachers   _____

2. Communicates needs, thoughts, and experiences   _____

3. Describes things and events verbally and nonverbally   _____

4. Responds to questions from classmates   _____

5. Uses new vocabulary in conversations   _____

6. Uses words to problem solve   _____

Comments:

_____
_____
_____
_____
_____
_____
_____

Student Name_____ Classroom_____

Teacher_____ Date_____

Math: Classifying

Key:

4 – always   **3 – sometimes**   **2 - rarely**   **1 – never**

1. Recognizes patterns   _____

2. Recognizes that patterns repeat   _____

3. Sorts items into sub-groups according to attribute (for example, by color, size, shape, or texture)   _____

4. Uses new math vocabulary in conversations   _____

5. Uses words to problem solve   _____

Comments:

_____
_____
_____
_____
_____
_____
_____
_____

3. **Checklist**

   If you want to assess skills—and not behaviors—many times you can use a checklist. Skills you can assess using a checklist usually are the learning goals that each state, state department of education, and accreditation agency list as learning objectives. Some of these objectives include:

   - Mathematics—number recognition; count concrete objects; shapes; patterns; listen to and says the names of numbers; describe and compare attributes; measurement
   - Science—name and use simple tools and equipment, record observations, ask questions, discuss observations with others, days of the week; seasons; plants, people and animals are alive; rocks are not alive
   - English Language Arts—letter recognition; letter sound recognition; recognize common types of texts; parts of a book; recognize first letter of name; write first letter of name; use dictating and drawing to tell a story
   - Health—brush teeth after meals in school; name healthy food choices; can name who to talk to about different kinds of problems (doctor, nurse, a parent, the teacher, policeman, fireman); cover mouth when coughing and sneezing; wash hands correctly know that medicines help you when you are sick

   When designing a checklist, make sure you organize it so that the items are listed in the order you expect them to happen. Remember, a checklist is not used to assess behaviors! Checklists are based on the learning goals as spelled out in your state regulations, in the curriculum frameworks, and in other learning guidelines from the department of education and accreditation agencies. These are the items you will write down on the checklist to assess the students. Be specific and avoid generalities when you write the list. For example, don't say, "Recognizes five letters of the alphabet." Instead say, "Recognizes the letters A, B, L, R, T."

Checklists are to be completed using a "Yes/No" or "Y/N" format. Sometimes you can be creative with word choices for filling in a checklist and use "Great/Oops!" (you do have freedom as you create,) but the teacher responses must be in the equivalent of the "yes/no" format.

Checklists help teachers to zoom in on areas where students might need some extra support. A checklist that is used to assess something that is observable is a more authentic assessment. Remember: always write in a comment at the bottom!

Save all the checklists for each student so you can show student growth and improvement over time.

Checklists are quick and easy to make. If you were going to create a checklist, for example, to assess and track students brushing their teeth, it might look something like this:

Student Name_____ Classroom_____

Teacher _____ Date _____

Tooth Brushing Checklist

I can brush my teeth! (with support from my teacher)

Here's how I do it, step by step:

1. I get toothbrush and toothpaste from designated area _____

2. I wait in line for turn at sink _____

3. I turn on the water _____

4. I moisten the toothbrush _____

5. I apply the appropriate amount of paste to brush _____

6. I brush my teeth appropriately _____

7. I rinse my teeth and keep it all in the sink _____

8. I rinse my toothbrush and cover the toothpaste tube _____

9. I wash my hands _____

10. I dry my hands _____

11. Paper towel in the trash _____

12. I shut off the water _____

13. I return the toothbrush and toothpaste to designated area _____

Comments:

_____
_____
_____
_____

7 The Learner with Special Needs

Special Learning Groups and Adapting the Curriculum

An accessible curriculum has all the children participating, regardless of any specialized need of a student. Teachers need to adapt their curriculum and lesson plans so that all of the children in the class are included, take part in the lesson, learn, and grow.

How do people learn?

Howard Gardner lists, in a paper he wrote in 2005 (pages 7-9) called "Multiple Lenses on the Mind," that there are eight possibly nine different types of intelligences and ways through which people learn best:

- Linguistic intelligence (writer, orator, journalist)
- Logical mathematical intelligence (mathematician, scientist)
- Musical intelligence (the capacity to create, perform, and appreciate music)
- Spatial intelligence (the capacity to solve problems or fashion products using your
whole body, or parts of your body like hands or mouth—exhibited by athletes, dancers, actors, craftspersons, surgeons
- Intraspersonal intelligence (capacity to understand oneself—strengths, weaknesses, fears)

- Naturalist intelligence (capacity to make consequential distinctions in nature—between one plant and another, among animals, clouds, mountains. Scientist Charles Darwin)
- Intelligence of big questions (when children ask about the size of the universe, when adults ponder death, love, conflict, the future of the planet)

Gardner feels that all of us have all of the eight or nine intelligences, but that no two individuals have exactly the same profile of intelligences. What does this mean to teachers?

We need to present the things we teach in different ways using different formats. A curriculum based on the Arts enables us to do that more easily than other types of curriculum.

Through the Arts we address musical intelligence (Music, Dance, Theater Arts), spatial intelligence (Dance and Theater Arts), linguistic intelligence (Theater Arts), logical and mathematical intelligences (Music, Visual Arts, Theater Arts). Through the Critique we accommodate students who may have a more intrapersonal intelligence. Through the Science Center activities our students observe, learn, and ask questions about nature and the natural environment. In everything we do, we encourage our students to ask the big questions.

How does this translate to lesson plans?

Teachers need to adapt their lesson plans to meet the learning needs of the their students. When you plan a lesson, make a quick note of things you can do to make it easier and things you can do to make it more complex. Some basic rules of thumb include:

- Break the learning down into smaller steps to make it more accessible to students who may be, for example, English language learners

- Take away steps for some students to make it easier. We want students to feel good about themselves and that they can succeed. A student who always feels as if they don't get it or can't do it will walk away, disengage, and feel badly about themselves.

- Add a few steps for other students to make it more complex. If a lesson is too easy for some students, they will walk away, disengage, not feel that they are a part of group, or a part of the class, or that they matter.

- Present things visually (show pictures) and orally (explain with words while you show students pictures)

- Have things for students to touch and hold as part of the lesson (while you explain with words and show pictures)

- Think of activities (often with a song) so that the students can move their bodies to help them learn

- Remember to repeat things. People learn through repetition

- Sometimes you need to give your students a little extra time (everyone learns at a different pace.) Other students are done in a flash—make sure you have extra things for these students to do, too. Keep everyone engaged, exploring, and learning!

8 The Long and Short

There is no other profession quite like teaching. I don't think any other job is as demanding, as low paying, or as rewarding as teaching. We plant the seeds and hope.

None of us will be there, on a rainy—sunny—cloudy—snowing day when something we said for the nine thousandth time is remembered, and that very small person now all grown up makes a better choice, ("Don't rush, take your time, stop and think,") remembers diplomacy, ("Say please and thank you. Look at how sad you've made Tara. She's crying because of what you said. You should apologize. We don't want to make people cry,") or turns away from violence, ("No guns in school. No hitting. Use your words.") That day will come—and it makes it all worthwhile.

YOU ARE
AN AWESOME TEACHER!

9 Blank Forms

Weekly Planning Grid

Teacher: Classroom: Dates:

	Monday	Tuesday	Wednesday	Thursday	Friday	
THEME:						
Arts Area & Concept	Dance	Visual Arts	Music	Theater Arts		
Literature						
Literacy & Language Building						
Writing Center						
Math Center						
Science Center						
Morning Activity						
Afternoon Activity						
Home and Family Connection						
Diversity Connection						
Story Telling: All About Me!						

Lesson Plan   Teacher: Classroom: Date:

Theme:

Art Area/Concept:

Literature:

Responding to Literature:

New Vocabulary:

AM/PM Circle Time:

AM Activity (Arts Area Center):

AM Math Center:

AM Science Center:

AM Writing Center:

PM Activity (Arts Area Center):

PM Math Center:

PM Science Center:

PM Writing Center:

Materials:

Lesson Plan   Teacher: Classroom: Date:

Theme:

Art Area/Concept:

Literature:

Responding to Literature:

New Vocabulary:

AM Circle Time:

AM Activity (Arts Area Center):

AM Math Center:

AM Science Center:

AM Writing Center:

Materials:

Lesson Plan   Teacher: Classroom: Date:

Theme:

Art Area/Concept:

Literature:

Responding to Literature:

New Vocabulary:

PM Circle Time:

PM Activity (Arts Area Center):

PM Math Center:

PM Science Center:

PM Writing Center:

Materials:

MATERIALS to Order

Teacher/Classroom: _____ Request Date: _____

For:	Center Has:	Need to Order*:
Monday		
Tuesday		
Wednesday		
Thursday		
Friday		

* If possible, please include price or price estimate

Dear Teacher:

In order for us to learn how well we are doing in achieving our goals, and to think about what we might want to do differently, we need feedback.

Thank you for taking the time to observe my lesson. If you can, try to spend a few minutes thinking about—and jotting down—what worked, what didn't go as smoothly as we would hope, and any suggestions you have for change.

Here is a form to make everything a little easier.

Thank you!

Date	Classroom	Observation	Observer

Student Name _____ **Classroom** _____

Activity _____

Students rate whether they liked or did not like an activity by indicating the corresponding smile face or frown face

APPENDIX 1

Supporting Documents:

The National Association for the Education of Young Children (NAEYC)

The National Association for the Education of Young Children (NAEYC)

I have used the following NAEYC documents to support my curriculum:

I **"Early Childhood Curriculum, Assessment, and Program Evaluation,"** based on the 2003 Joint Position Statement of the National Association for the Education of Young Children (NAEYC) and the National Association of Early Childhood Specialists in State Departments of Education (NAECS/SDE):

The Position:
- Construct comprehensive systems of curriculum, assessment, and program evaluation
- A set of core principles and values
- Belief in civic and democratic values
- Support children as individuals and members of families, cultures, and communities
- Partnerships with families
- Shared accountability
- Implement curriculum that is thoughtfully planned, challenging, engaging, developmentally appropriate, culturally and linguistically responsive, comprehensive, and likely to promote positive outcomes for all young children
- Assessments—ethical, appropriate, valid, and reliable—a central part of all early childhood programs
- Assess strengths, progress, and needs
- Assessment methods to be developmentally appropriate, culturally and linguistically responsive, tied to children's daily activities, supported by professional development, inclusive of families, connected to specific, beneficial purposes: (1) making sound decisions about teaching and learning, (2) identifying significant concerns that may require focused intervention for individual children, and (3) helping programs improve their educational and developmental interventions
- Regular program evaluation—guided by program goals and using varied, appropriate, conceptually and technically sound evidence, to determine the extent to which programs meet the expected standards of quality and to examine intended as well as unintended results

Position Statements' Intended Effects:
Take informed positions on significant, controversial issues affecting young children's education and development—in this case, issues related to curriculum development and implementation, the purposes and uses of assessment data, and benefits and risks in accountability systems for early childhood programs

Promote broad-based dialogue on these issues within and beyond the early childhood field

Create a shared language and evidence-based frame of reference so that practitioners, decision makers, and families may talk together about early childhood curriculum, assessment, and program evaluation and their relationship to early learning standards and program standards

Influence public policies—in this case, those related to early childhood curriculum development, adoption, and implementation; child assessment practices; and program evaluation practices—one by one as these fit together into a coherent educational system linked to child outcomes or standards.

Stimulate investments needed to create accessible, affordable, high-quality learning environments and professional development that support the implementation of excellent early childhood curriculum, assessment, and program evaluation

Build more satisfying experiences and better educational and developmental outcomes for all young children

Indicators of Effectiveness:
- Children are active and engaged
- Goals are clear and shared by all
- Curriculum is evidence-based
- Valid content is learned through investigation, play, and focused, intentional teaching
- Curriculum builds on prior learning and experiences
- Curriculum is comprehensive (encompasses critical areas of development including children's physical well-being and motor development; social and emotional development; approaches to learning; language development; cognition and general knowledge; and subject matter areas such as science, mathematics, language, literacy, social studies, and the arts
- Professional standards validate the curriculum's subject-matter content
- The curriculum is likely to benefit children

Assessment of Young Children:
- ❑ Assessment to support learning and instruction
- ❑ Assessment to identify children who may need additional services

Assessment methods include
- Observation
- Documentation of children's work
- Checklists and rating scales
- Portfolios

Assess:
- Strengths
- Developmental status
- Progress
- Needs

Things that may negatively impact an assessment:
- Assessment is directed toward a narrow set of skills
- Poor quality or poorly administered assessments
- Anxiety (child's)
- Hunger (child's)
- Inability to understand the language or instructions (child's)
- Culturally learned hesitation in initiating conversations with adults

Program Evaluation and Accountability:
- Evaluation is used for continuous improvement
- Goals become guides for evaluation (the program/curriculum goals) intended and unintended
- Comprehensive goals are used (include goals related to families, teachers and other staff, community, as well as child-centered goals that address a broad set of developmental and learning outcomes
- Evaluations use a valid design
- Multiple sources of data are available (including program data, child demographic data, information about staff qualifications, administrative practices, classroom quality assessments, implementation data, and other information that provides a context for interpreting the results of child assessments)

Curriculum:
Curriculum is thoughtfully planned: Whatever the children's ages, curriculum goals link with important developmental tasks and are comprehensive in scope. Teaching strategies are tailored to children's ages, developmental capacities, language and culture, and abilities or

disabilities. A major shift as children move into kindergarten and the primary grades is toward greater focus on subject matter areas, without ignoring their developmental foundations.

Preschoolers:
- Goals focus on children's exploration, inquiry, and expanding vocabularies
- Goals address children's physical well-being and motor development; social and emotional development; approaches to learning; language development; and cognition and general knowledge
- Experiences provide for knowledge and skill learning in literacy, mathematics, science, social studies, and the visual and performing arts

Curriculum that is challenging and engaging: For all ages the curriculum leads children from where they are to new accomplishments while maintaining their interest and active involvement. Content that is engaging for children of different ages changes with development and new experiences, requiring careful observation and adaptation.

Preschoolers:
- Curriculum facilitates children's construction of knowledge through their interactions with materials, each other, and adults.
- Curriculum provides experiences in which children's thinking moves from the simple to the complex, from the concrete to the abstract.
- Curriculum provides opportunities for children to initiate activities, as well as for teacher initiation and scaffolding.
- Curriculum leads to children's recognition of their own achievements

Curriculum that is developmentally appropriate and culturally and linguistically responsive: Whatever the children's ages, curriculum fits well with their developmental levels, abilities and disabilities, individual characteristics, families and communities, and cultural contexts. Curriculum supports educational equity for children who are learning a second language. Curriculum for younger children makes cultural connections primarily through relationships, daily routines, and "rituals"; older children benefit from more explicit incorporation of culturally relevant materials and from topic-centered as well as integrated learning opportunities

II **The NAEYC "All Criteria Document,"** (2012) Updated 01/10/2012. This is a document used when evaluating preschools and centers for accreditation by NAEYC. I have used the following standards:

Standard One: Relationships

1.A. - Building Positive Relationships among Teachers and Families

1.A.01a; 1.A.03a, b; 1.A.05a
Teachers work in partnership with families—regular ongoing, two-way communication

1.A.02a
Teachers will gain info about the ways families define their own race, religion, home language, culture, and family structure

1.B. – Building Positive Relationships between Teachers and Children

1.B.01a; 1.B.02a; 1.B.03a, b; 1.B.05a, b, c, d; 1.B.06a
Teaching Staff will—foster children's emotional well being (respect for children, creating a positive emotional climate.)

1.B.06a
Provide support for children's appropriate expressions of emotion both positive (joy, pleasure, excitement,) and negative (anger, frustration, sadness.)

1.B.07a, b, c, d, e
Teachers evaluate and change their responses based on individual needs. Teachers vary their interactions to be sensitive and responsive to differing abilities, temperaments, activity levels, cognitive and social development

1.B.08a
Teachers support children's competent and self-reliant exploration and use of classroom materials

1.B.09a
Never use physical punishment such as shaking or hitting and do not engage in psychological abuse or coercion

1.B.10a
Never use threats or derogatory remarks; never withhold or threaten to withhold food as a form of discipline

1.B.11a, b, c
Talk frequently with children, listen to children with attention and respect; respond to children's questions and requests; use strategies to

communicate effectively and build relationships with every child; engage regularly in meaningful and extended conversations with each child

Standard Two: Curriculum

2.A. – Curriculum: Essential Characteristics

2.A.01a
...uses one or more written curricula or curriculum frameworks consistent with its philosophy that addresses central aspects of child development

2.A.02a
A clearly stated curriculum or curriculum framework provides a coherent focus for planning children's experiences. It allows for adaptations and modifications to ensure access to the curriculum for all children

2.A.03.a
Curriculum guides teachers' development and intentional implementation of learning opportunities consistent with the program's goals and objectives

2.A.04a, b
Curriculum can be implemented in a manner that reflects responsiveness to family home values, beliefs, experiences, and language

2.A.05a
Curriculum goals and objectives guide teachers' ongoing assessment of children's progress

2.A.06a
Curriculum guides teachers to integrate assessment information with curriculum goals to individualize learning

2.A08a, b, c, d, (then materials and equipment:)e, f, g, h, i, j, k
Materials and equipment used to implement curriculum reflect the lives of the children and families as well as the diversity found in society including: gender diversity, age diversity, language diversity, and diversity of abilities

Materials and equipment provide for children's safety while being appropriately challenging; encourage exploration, experimentation, and discovery; promote action and interaction; are organized to support independent use; are rotated to reflect changing curriculum and accommodate new interests and skill levels; are rich in variety; accommodate children's special needs

2.A.10a, b, c, d, e, f
Curriculum guides teachers to incorporate content, concepts, and activities that foster social development, emotional development, physical development, language development, cognitive development, and integrate key areas of content including literacy, mathematics, science, technology, creative expression and the arts, health & safety, and social studies

2.A.12a
Curriculum guides teachers to plan for children's engagement in play (including dramatic play and blocks) that is integrated into classroom topics of study

2.B. – Areas of Development: Social-Emotional Development

2.B.01a, b, c
Children have varied opportunities to engage throughout the day with teaching staff who are attentive and responsive to them; facilitate their social competence; facilitate their ability to learn through interacting with other

2.B.02a, b
Children have varied opportunities to recognize and name their own and others' feelings

2.B.04a
Children have varied opportunities to develop a sense of competence and positive attitudes toward learning such as persistence, engagement, curiosity, and mastery

2.B.05a
Children have varied opportunities to develop skills for entering into social groups, developing friendships, learning to help, and other pre-social behavior
(this is opportunities for independent not staff supported—e.g. multiple group clean-ups)

2.B.06a, b, c
Children have varied opportunities to interact positively, respectfully, and cooperatively with others; learn from and with one another; resolve conflicts in constructive ways

The Preschool Curriculum Handbook

2.B.07a
Children have varied opportunities to learn to understand, empathize with and take into account other people's perspectives

2.D. – Language Development

2.D.01a, b, c
Children are provided with opportunities for language acquisition that align with the program philosophy; consider family perspectives; consider community perspectives

2.D.02a
Children are provided opportunities to experience oral and written communication in a language their family uses or understands

2.D.03a, b, c
Children have varied opportunities to develop competence in verbal and non-verbal communication by responding to questions; communicating needs, thoughts, and experiences; describing things and events

2.D.04a, b, c, d
Children have varied opportunities to develop vocabulary through conversations; experiences, field trips; and books

2.E. – Curriculum Content Area for Cognitive Development: Early Literacy

2.E.03a, b, c, d
Children have opportunities to become familiar with print. They are actively involved in making sense out of print and they have opportunities to become familiar with, recognize, and use print that is accessible throughout the classroom: items belonging to a child are labeled with his or her name; materials are labeled; print is used to describe some rules and routines (e.g. hand washing instructions); teachers help children recognize print and connect it to spoken word.

2.E.04a, b, c, d, e, f, g, h, i
Children have varied opportunities to: be read books in an engaging manner in group or individualized settings at least twice a day in full-day programs and at least once daily in half-day programs; be read to regularly in individualized ways including one-to-one or in small groups of two to six; explore books on their own and have places that are conducive to the quiet enjoyment of books; have access to various types of books including storybooks, factual books, books with rhymes, alphabet books, and wordless books; be read the same book

on repeated occasions; retell and re-enact events in storybooks; engage in conversations that help them understand the content of the book; be assisted in linking books to other aspects of the curriculum; identify the parts of books and differentiate print from pictures

2.E.05a, b, c, d, e, f, g
Children have multiple and varied opportunities to write: writing materials and activities are readily available in art, dramatic play, and other learning centers learning centers anywhere in classroom and outdoors, too, e.g. book corner, block area, dramatic play center—WRITING MATERIALS MUST BE PRESENT IN AT LEAST TWO LEARNING CENTERS—various types of writing are supported including scribbling, letter-like marks, and developmental spelling; children have daily opportunities to write or dictate their ideas; children are provided needed assistance in writing the words and messages they are trying to communicate; Children are given the support they need to write on their own including access to the alphabet; to printed words about topics of current interest; both of which are made available at eye level or on laminated cards: children see teaching staff model functional use of writing and are helped to discuss the many ways writing is used in daily life

2.E.07a, b
Children are given opportunities to: recognize and: write letters

2.E.08a, b
Children have access to: books throughout the classroom and; writing materials throughout the classroom

2.F. – Curriculum Content Area for Cognitive Development: Early Mathematics

2.F.02a
Children are provided varied opportunities and materials to build an understanding of numbers, number names, and their relationship to object quantities and to symbols

2.F.03a
Children are provided varied opportunities and materials to categorize by one or two attributes such as shape, size, color

2.F.04a
Children are provided varied opportunities and materials that encourage them to integrate mathematical terms into everyday conversation

2.F.06a, b
Children are provided varied opportunities and materials that help them understand the concept of measurement by using standard; and non-standard units of measurement

2.F.06a
Children are provided varied opportunities and materials to understand basic concepts of geometry by, for example, naming and recognizing two- and three-dimensional shapes and recognizing how figures are composed of different shapes

2.F.07a
Children are provided varied opportunities and materials that help them recognize and naming repeating patterns such as: sequence of colors, shapes, or sounds or other attributes that occur again and again

2.G. – Curriculum Content Area for Cognitive Development: Science

2.G.02a b, c
Children are provided varied opportunities and materials to learn key content and principles of science such as: the difference between living and nonliving things (e.g. plants versus rocks) and life cycles of various organisms (e.g. plants, butterflies, humans); earth and sky (e.g. seasons, weather, geologic features, light and shadow, sun, moon, and stars); structure and property of matter (e.g. characteristics that include concepts such as hard and soft, floating and sinking) and behavior of materials (e.g. transformation of liquids and solids by dissolving or melting)

2.G.03a
Children are provided varied opportunities and materials that encourage them to use the five senses to observe, explore, and experiment with scientific phenomena

2.G.04a
Children are provided varied opportunities to use simple tools to observe objects and scientific phenomena

2.G.05a, b
Children are provided varied opportunities and materials to: collect data and to; represent and document their findings (e.g. through drawing or graphing)

2.G.06a
Children are provided varied opportunities and materials that encourage them to think, question, and reason about observed and inferred phenomena

2.G.08a
Children are provided varied opportunities and materials that help them learn and use scientific terminology and vocabulary associated with content areas

2.J. – Curriculum Content Area for Cognitive Development: Creative Expression and Appreciation for the Arts

2.J.01a, b, c, d
Children are provided varied opportunities to gain appreciation of: art in ways that reflect cultural diversity; music in ways that reflect cultural diversity; drama in ways that reflect cultural diversity; dance in ways that reflect cultural diversity

2.J.04a, b, c, d
Children are provided varied opportunities to learn new concepts and vocabulary related to: art; music; drama, and; dance

2.J.05a
Children are provided varied opportunities to develop and widen their repertoire of skills that support artistic expression

2.J.06a, b, c, d
Children are provided many and varied open-ended opportunities and materials to express themselves creatively through: music; drama; dance and; two-dimensional and three-dimensional art

2.J.07a, b
Children have opportunities to respond to the art of: other children and; adults

2.K. – Curriculum Content Area for Cognitive Development: Health and Safety

2.K.02a, b, c, d, e
Children are provided varied opportunities and materials to help them learn about nutrition, including: identifying sources of food; recognizing; preparing; eating, and; valuing healthy foods.

2.K.03a, b
Children are provided varied opportunities and materials that increase their awareness of safety rules in their: classroom; home, and community

2.K.04a
Children have opportunities to practice safety procedures.

2.L. – Curriculum Content Area for Cognitive Development: Social Studies

2.L.01a, b
Children are provided varied learning opportunities that foster positive identity and an emerging sense of: self and; others

2.L.02a
Children are offered opportunities to become a part of the classroom community so that each child feels accepted and gains a sense of belonging

2.L.03a, b, c, d, e, f
Children are provided varied opportunities and materials to build their understanding of diversity in non-stereotypical ways in: culture; family structure; ability; language; age; gender

2.L.05a
Children are provided varied opportunities and materials to learn about the community in which they live

2.L.06a, b, c, d, e
Children have varied opportunities to engage in discussions about: fairness; friendship; responsibility; authority; differences

2.L.07a
Children are provided varied opportunities and materials to learn about physical characteristics of their local environment as a foundation for learning geography

2.L.08a, b
Children are provided varied opportunities and materials to learn how people affect their environment in: positive and; negative ways

2.L.09a
Children are provided opportunities and materials that build a foundation for understanding economic concepts (e.g. playing restaurant, managing a store, and identifying and exchanging money)

STANDARD 3: Teaching

3.E. – Responding to Children's Interests and Needs

3.E.03a
Teachers use children's interest in and curiosity about the world to engage them with new content and developmental skills (may include show and tell activities, anecdotal notes, newsletters showing that teaching staff decided to do a unit or study a topic because of a child's interest in the topic—dinosaurs, space, birds, snow, new babies, etc.)

3.E.04a
Teachers use their knowledge of individual children to modify strategies and materials to enhance children's learning (include written evidence in lesson planning and documentation with anecdotal notes about individuals or individual child assessments)

3.F. – Making Learning Meaningful

3.F.01a
Teachers use curriculum in all content and developmental areas as a flexible framework for teaching and to support the development of daily plans and learning experiences

3.F.03a
Teachers and families work together to help children participate successfully in the early childhood setting when professional values and practices differ from family values and practices. *Written evidence could include parent/teacher conferences; questionnaires and intake sheets for families about their culture; and resources for teachers and staff to help them communicate with families about cultural differences and implement culturally responsive service plans and practices.*

3.F.04a, b, c
Teaching staff help children understand spoken language, (particularly when children a learning a new language) by using: pictures; familiar objects; body language, and physical cues. *Evidence includes things such as picture collections, labels on materials, narration and naming by teaching staff of routines and the materials involved in routines, and child dictations*

The Preschool Curriculum Handbook

STANDARD 4: Assessment of Child Progress

4.A. – Creating an Assessment Plan

4.A.01a
Programs conduct assessments as an integral part of the program. Programs use assessments to support children's learning, using a variety of methods such as observations, checklists, rating scales, and individually administered tests.

4.A.02a, b, c, d, e
The program has a written plan for assessment that describes assessment purposes, procedures, and uses of the results. The plan also includes: conditions under which children will be assessed; timelines associated with assessments that occur throughout the year; procedures to keep individual child records confidential; ways to involve families in planning and implementing assessments; methods to effectively communicate assessment information to families.

4.B. – Using Appropriate Assessment Methods

4.B.05a, b, c, d, e, f
Staff developed assessment methods: are aligned with curriculum goals; provide an accurate picture of all children's abilities and progress; are appropriate and valid for their stated purposes; provide meaningful and stable results for all learners, including English-language learners and children with special needs; provide teachers with clear ideas for curriculum development and daily planning; are regularly reviewed to be certain that they are providing the needed information.

Child portfolios are a common staff-developed assessment method. Self-developed assessment methods may also include observation forms, checklists, or rating scales designed by the teaching staff.

III *Positive Outcomes for Children with Disabilities: Recommendations for Curriculum, Assessment, and Program Evaluation,* developed by the Division for Early Childhood of the Council for Exceptional Children, endorsed by the National Association for the Education of Young Children, March 2007.

Curriculum
Key Recommendation:
To benefit all children, including those with disabilities and developmental delays, it is important to implement an integrated,

developmentally appropriate, universally designed curriculum framework that is flexible, comprehensive, and linked to assessment and program evaluation activities. Such a curriculum framework can help ensure successful access, which in turn facilitates participation and learning of all children and families regardless of need, ability, or background. A comprehensive curriculum framework encompasses four elements: assessment; scope and sequence; activities and intervention strategies; and progress monitoring. A curriculum framework is a dynamic system that should guide all aspects of a high quality program.

Key Issues in Curriculum for Young Children with Disabilities:
The purpose of this section is to describe a comprehensive curriculum framework that is built on the principles of universal design as a means of ensuring access, participation, and progress for all learners. Further, a curriculum framework as described here provides a set of recommended practices for (a) promoting active engagement and learning; (b) individualizing and adapting practices for each child based on ongoing data; (c) providing opportunities for children's learning within regular routines; and (d) working collaboratively and sharing responsibilities among families and professionals (Sandall et al, 2005).

Universal design for learning.
The 2004 amendments to IDEA require that all children, regardless of ability, have access to the general curriculum, and have the opportunity to participate and make progress in the general curriculum. While the mandate is not new, many providers working with young children continue to struggle with understanding how to make each component of the mandate a reality.

An accessible curriculum means that all aspects of the curriculum (i.e., the environment, the goals, the content, the instructional methods and interactions, the assessments, and the toys/materials) invite active participation of all children, regardless of disability or special needs.

There are three essential principles of universal design for learning that have been identified (Blackhurst et al., 1999; CAST, 2004; Orkwis, 1999; Orkwis & McLane, 1998). A universally designed curriculum framework provides:

• Multiple means of representation. This principle ensures instruction, questions, expectations, and learning opportunities are provided in various formats and at different levels of complexity, addressing a range of ability levels and visual, auditory, and kinesthetic needs.

(This principle is reflected in the activities listed in Table 1A in the Appendix.)
• Multiple means of engagement. This principle ensures various opportunities are presented for arousing children's attention, curiosity, and motivation, addressing a wide range of interests, preferences, and personal styles. Engagement is then maintained by providing various levels of scaffolding, repetition, and appropriate challenges to ensure successful learning. (This principle is reflected in the activities listed in Table 1B in the Appendix.)
• Multiple means of expression. This principle ensures children have a variety of formats for responding, demonstrating what they know, and for expressing ideas, feelings, and preferences. In addition, children have options in their use of resources, toys, and materials, addressing individual strengths, preferences, and abilities. (This principle is reflected in the activities listed in Table 1C in the Appendix.)

The specific elements of a cohesive, universally designed curriculum framework include assessment and progress monitoring, scope and sequence strategies, and activities and intervention strategies; these elements also require collaboration with other members of the team. These specific elements, described more fully in the following section, must also take into consideration universal design for learning, the essential need of partnering, and an understanding that providers will need to be flexible when implementing a curriculum framework, and provide accommodations and modification as needed.

Assessment and progress monitoring.
It is important that teams conduct comprehensive, universally designed, and authentic assessment and ongoing monitoring of all children's development and learning. Team members need a clear understanding of all children's current skills and abilities to ensure access and participation, and to develop appropriate learning opportunities

Indicators of Effectiveness

Multiple means of representation are provided so that the curriculum is accessible to all children regardless of ability, needs, or background

An example of a curriculum framework with multiple means of representation is one where adults use practices such as differentiated instruction and the development of learning opportunities at different levels of complexity. For instance, the teacher gives children options for learning about the moon from a collection of books that range from easy to difficult, videos, Internet sites, models, or planetarium visits. These options accommodate a range of ability levels as well as visual, auditory, and kinesthetic needs. Further, since some children may do better when they hear information while others need to see it, adults should provide multi-sensory options in different formats, such as giving instructions with both words and pictures. For example, a daily schedule can be written, and pictures or objects can be provided for children with visual impairments.

Multiple means of expression are supported so that children can demonstrate what they know and are able to do regardless of ability, needs, or background.
A flexible curriculum framework encourages all children to communicate and show what they know and are able to do using any method they can or prefer. In general, children should be encouraged to use a variety of verbal and non-verbal expressions to demonstrate the skills and concepts they have acquired, those that are emerging, and those that team members need to continue to support and provide practice opportunities for. Adults should encourage and support any form of expression, including the use of speech, signs, gestures, pictures, objects, writing, art, and assistive technology. By allowing children to express themselves in multiple ways, children will have greater independence and success in getting their wants and needs met and in sharing their ideas.

Programs adopt curriculum goals that are clear and shared by all.
common goals (also referred to as outcomes or standards) should stem from critical concepts and skills deemed important for all young children to acquire (i.e., for children with disabilities, children at risk, and children without identified disabilities). At times, particular children may need more individualized goals (often identified on an individualized family service plan/individualized education plan). Individualized plans help team members address the possible reasons a child is having difficulty accessing and participating in daily activities and routines and making progress toward the common goals in the general curriculum. Individualized needs for children should represent underlying, earlier, or prerequisite concepts and skills that once obtained will enhance a child's access, participation, and progress in daily activities and the general curriculum

Curriculum is comprehensive.
Programs should have a curriculum framework that is well understood by all stakeholders and covers all areas of growth and development considered important for young children, and one that addresses federal, state, or agency standards

Assessment

Key Recommendation

Assessment is a shared experience between families and professionals in which information and ideas are exchanged to benefit a child's growth and development. Assessment practices should be integrated and individualized in order to: (a) answer the questions posed by the assessment team (including family members); (b) integrate the child's everyday routines, interests, materials, caregivers, and play partners within the assessment process; and (c) develop a system for shared partnerships with professionals and families for the communication and collection of ongoing information valuable for teaching and learning. Therefore, assessment teams should implement a child- and family-centered, team-based, and ecologically valid assessment process. This process should be designed to address each child's unique strengths and needs through authentic, developmentally appropriate, culturally and linguistically responsive, multidimensional assessment methods. The methods should be matched to the purpose for the assessment, linked to curriculum and intervention, and supported by professional development.

Family centered and team based process.
Families contribute to the assessment process in multiple ways. Families:
• Enhance team observations by describing their child's performance in other settings;
• Suggest options, activities, and materials for interaction;
• Facilitate child engagement

Families not only support their child during the assessment process but also validate the findings suggested by other team members, identify discrepancies in performance, report on typical patterns of behavior, and co-assess with team members to ensure the best performance by their child.

APPENDIX 2

Supporting Documents:

The Massachusetts Department of Early Education and Care (MA DEEC)

The Massachusetts Department of Early Education and Care (MA DEEC)

I have used the following MA DEEC documents to support my curriculum:

I   **606 CMR: DEPARTMENT OF EARLY EDUCATION AND CARE**

606 CMR 7.00: Standards for the Licensure or Approval of Family Child Care; Small Group and School Age and Large Group and School Age Child Care Programs

7.05: Interactions Among Adults and Children

The following requirements apply to all programs, including family child care, small group and school age and large group and school age child care.

(1) Educators must be responsive to children's individual needs and support the development of self-esteem, self-expression, autonomy, social competence, and school readiness.

(2) Educators must be nurturing and responsive to children by:

> (a) frequently expressing warmth to individual children through behaviors such as holding babies. social conversations (including response to babies' vocalizations), joint laughter, eye contact, and smiles, and communicating at children's eye level;

> (b) providing attentive, consistent, comforting, and culturally sensitive care;

> (c) being consistent and predictable in their physical and emotional care of children, and when implementing program rules and expectations;

> (d) recognizing signs of stress in children's behavior and responding with appropriate stress-reducing activities.

(3) Educators must support children in the development of self-esteem, independence, and self-regulation by:

> (a) demonstrating courtesy and respect when interacting with children and adults;

(b) encouraging appropriate expression of emotions, both positive *(e.g.* joy, pleasure, excitement) and negative *(e.g.,* anger, frustration and sadness);

(c) providing opportunities for children to develop self-help skills as they are ready; encouraging children's efforts, work and accomplishments;

(d) assuring that all children have equal opportunities to take part in all activities and use all materials;

(e) offering opportunities for children to make choices and decisions.

(4) Educators must support children in the development of social competence by:
- (a) promoting interaction and language use among children and between children and adults by talking to and with children frequently;
- (b) encouraging children to share experiences and ideas;
- (c) modeling cooperation, problem-solving strategies and responsible behavior for children;
- (d) assisting children in learning social skills such as sharing, taking turns, and working together;
- (e) encouraging children to listen to, help, and support each other;
- (f) providing guidance to assist children in resolving conflicts, finding solutions to problems, and making decisions.
- (g) helping children to understand and respect people different from themselves;
- (h) helping children learn to respect each other's possessions and work;

(8) The following practices are strictly prohibited:
- (a) spanking or other corporal punishment of children;
- (b) subjecting children to cruel or severe punishment such as humiliation, verbal or physical abuse, neglect, or abusive treatment including any type of physical hitting inflicted in any manner upon the body, shaking, threats, or derogatory remarks;
- (c) depriving children of outdoor time, meals or snacks; force-feeding children or otherwise making them eat against their will, or in any way using food as a consequence;
- (d) disciplining a child for soiling, wetting, or not using the toilet; forcing a child to remain in soiled clothing or to remain on the toilet, or using any other unusual or excessive practices for toileting;

(e) confining a child to a swing, high chair, crib, playpen or any other piece of equipment for an extended period of time in *lieu* of supervision; and

f) excessive time-out. Time-out may not exceed one minute for each year of the child's age and must take place within an educator's view.

7.06: Curriculum and Progress Reports

The following requirements apply to all programs, including family child care, small group and school age and large group and school age child care.

(1) Curriculum.
(a) The licensee must provide a well-balanced curriculum. of specific, planned learning experiences that support the social, emotional, physical, intellectual and language development of all children. The curriculum must:

1. Be developmentally and linguistically appropriate
2. Provide for the development, interests, and temperaments of individual children
3. Support school readiness and/or educational development
4. Include goals for the knowledge and skills to be acquired by children in the areas of English language arts, mathematics, science and technology/engineering, history and social sciences, comprehensive health, and the arts

(b) The licensee must have evidence of a plan describing how program activities support and engage children through specific learning experiences. Such plan must be appropriate to the ages and development of the children served, to the length of the program day and to the program objectives. As appropriate children must participate in the development of the plan, and the plan must provide for:

1. Reasonable regularity in routine, with sufficient flexibility to respond to the needs of individual children and to capitalize on unscheduled learning opportunities.
2. Opportunities for children to have a free choice among a variety of activities or to play alone or with one or several chosen peers, if desired, for at least half the program day

3. Opportunities for children to participate in a variety of creative activities, such as art, music, literature, dramatic play and science, encouraging exploration, experimentation, and discovery
6. Opportunities for children of all ages to interact with peers and adults to develop competence in verbal and nonverbal communication by responding to questions; communicating needs, thoughts, and experiences, and describing things and events
7. Educators reading books daily with children of all ages in an engaging manner in group or individual settings
10. Opportunities to explore issues of cultural, social, and individual diversity while developing awareness, acceptance, and appreciation of differences such as gender, language, culture, ethnicity, family composition, and differing abilities
11. Learning experiences that support problem solving, critical thinking, communication, language and literacy development, social skills and relationship building
12. Opportunities to learn about proper nutrition, good health, and personal safety
13. Specific reasonable accommodations to allow children with disabilities to participate in regular program activities whenever possible

(3) Progress Reports.
A written progress report must be prepared periodically on the progress of each child in the program. The program must offer parents a conference to discuss the content of the report. A copy of the progress report must be given to the parent and a copy kept in the child's record.

(a) Frequency.
1. For infants and children with identified special needs the progress reports must be prepared every three months
2. For toddlers and preschoolers, the progress reports must be prepared every six months.
3. For school age children, the progress reports must be prepared at least annually, at the midpoint of the child's program year.

(b) Content
The progress report must be based on observations and documentation of the child's progress in a range of activities over time and may include samples of the child's work.

1. For children younger than school age, the progress report must address the development and growth of the child including but not limited to the developmental domains of Cognitive, Social-Emotional, Language, and Fine and Gross Motor and Life Skills.
2. For school age children, the progress report must address the child's growth and development within the parameters of the program's statement of purpose.

(c) All Educators, specialists, and consultants working with the child in the program must be offered an opportunity to contribute to the progress report of the child.

II   **The MA DEEC Center and School Based QRIS Standards (Revised 12/14/2010):**

Category 1: Curriculum and Learning
Subcategories within Curriculum and Learning:
1A. Curriculum, Assessment, and Diversity
1B. Teacher-Child Relationships and Interactions

Curriculum And Learning: **1A. Curriculum, Assessment, and Diversity**
Level 1
Meets licensing regulations or non-licensable or license exempt and meets DEEC licensing requirements

Level 2
Materials reflect the language and culture of the children in the classroom, their communities, and represent the diversity of society.

Level 3
Staff include parental input in the progress reports. Program uses screening tools, progress reports, formative assessments, and information gathered through observation to set goals for individual children across all developmental domains.

Staff demonstrate language and literacy skills either in English or the child's language that provide a model for children.

Level 4
Program uses a curriculum that is aligned with MA guidelines for Preschool Learning Standards

Curriculum and Learning: **1B. Teacher-Child Relationships and Interactions**

Level 3
Staff engage children in meaningful conversations, use open-ended questions and provide opportunities throughout the day to scaffold their language to support the development of more complex receptive and expressive language, support children's use of language to share ideas, problem solve and have positive peer interactions.

Level 4
Staff utilize teaching strategies that ensure a positive classroom environment, engage children in learning and promote critical thinking skills.

Category 4: FAMILY AND COMMUNITY ENGAGEMENT

Level 3
A daily two way communication system is available between the educators and families through a variety of means. Families are encouraged to volunteer in the program, to assist in the classroom, and share cultural and language traditions or other interests such as their jobs, hobbies and other relevant information.

APPENDIX 3

Supporting Documents:

Massachusetts Department of Elementary and Secondary Education (MA DESE)

The Massachusetts Department of Elementary and Secondary Education (MA DESE)

I have used the following MA DESE documents to support my curriculum:

I   *Early Childhood Program Standards for Three and Four Year Olds (2003)*

Area 2: Curriculum and Assessment

Purpose: Curriculum is defined as **everything staff do with children**. A well-balanced curriculum supports the development of all children socially, emotionally, physically, and intellectually. The curriculum should be designed for active involvement by children in the learning process, recognizing that young children learn through play, active manipulation of the environment, concrete experiences, and communicating with peers and adults. The curriculum should provide a variety of activities and materials to encourage behaviors appropriate to each child's age, background, stage of development, and individual needs, including adaptations for children with disabilities.

Assessment is defined as the process of observing, recording, and documenting children's development, participation, and learning over time. The purpose of assessment is to help teachers plan appropriate activities for each child. Assessment should be ongoing, systematic, extracted from natural play activities, and cumulative.

B. The curriculum is BASED ON INFORMATION ABOUT THE CHILDREN derived from a variety of sources

>1. Child Observation: Observations of each child's development and learning are written and compiled systematically on an ongoing basis.
>2. Evaluation of Children's Progress: Observations may consist of anecdotal records, ongoing classroom and playground observations, checklists, and dated compilations of children's work (portfolios).
>3. Information Sharing: Information is shared regularly between parents and staff. Staff protect the confidentiality of information about children and families. (Conversations about an individual child should not be conducted in the presence of the child or any child or adult unrelated to the child.)

D. Activities, materials, and equipment promote EDUCATIONAL GOALS through concrete learning
    1. Learning experiences support problem solving, critical thinking, communication, and social skills within a meaningful context for the child.
    2. Play experiences foster development and organization of knowledge about the world around them.
    3. There are goals for social/emotional development, cognitive development, English language and literacy development, development of mathematical concepts, development of scientific concepts, self-expression in art, music, movement and dance, dramatic play, health, and physical development

E. Goals are adapted to meet INDIVIDUAL NEEDS
    1. Curriculum goals and activities are based on the individual needs and interests of the children enrolled, allowing for a range of abilities.
    2. Each child is viewed as a unique person with an individual pattern of development, interests, preferences.
    3. Choices of activities are always offered.
    4. Experiences are provided that help children increase their knowledge of other children's family traditions and foods, where appropriate.
    7. Requiring completion of closed-ended paper and pencil/crayon tasks are not encouraged.

L. There is opportunity for PARENTAL INPUT into curriculum
    1. There is a procedure for allowing parental input in the program's curriculum (e.g., a questionnaire or survey; parent group meetings, etc.).
    2. Parents are offered opportunities to increase their child observation skills and to share information with staff about their own observations of their child that will help staff in planning learning experiences.

Area 4: Family Involvement
Purpose: The program will invite parent involvement. Staff will engage in a supportive partnership around the child, program, and home to build mutual understanding and consistency for the child. Staff will support parent(s) as the primary educators of their child and will be respectful of the home and culture. Staff and parents will keep each other well informed about the child and program.

E. There are opportunities for PARENT PARTICIPATION

1. Parents and other family members are welcomed and encouraged to be involved in the program in various ways (e.g., serving as volunteers, participating on local early childhood council, attending parent meetings, serving on a curriculum development committee; toy lending libraries).
2. The program permits unannounced visits by parents while their child is present.
3. The program has a process for parents to provide input in the development of program policy and programming.

F. There are mechanisms in place for PARENT/STAFF COMMUNICATION

1. There is a verbal and/or written system of communication in the parent's preferred language, when reasonable, for sharing information between staff and parents.
2. Changes in a child's physical or emotional state, special problems or significant developments are brought to the parent's attention as soon as they arise.
3. Parents are informed about the program through regular means such as newsletters, postings on bulletin boards, frequent notes, telephone calls and other similar measures.

G. There are REPORTS AND CONFERENCES offered to parents

1. At least twice a year the program develops a written report on the educational and developmental progress of each child to be discussed with parent(s) at a conference, if possible.
2. Conferences are offered at least every six months, or as requested by parents, to discuss the child's progress at home and at the program.
3. For children with disabilities, reports are required every 3 months.
4. Parents are provided with a copy of the progress report and a copy is maintained in the child's folder.
5. Reports are disseminated only with the written consent of the parent(s).

II *Guidelines for Preschool Learning Experiences* (2003)

1. **All young children are capable of learning.** All children are capable of positive developmental outcomes. Preschool teachers should hold high expectations for all young children.

2. Children show individual differences in development. Although children develop skills and competencies through a generally predictable sequence of milestones, they do not develop them in exactly the same way or at exactly the same time. Some children may have a developmental delay or disability that requires individualized expectations, experiences, and materials.

3. Knowledge of child growth and development is essential for program development and implementation. Decisions about appropriate curriculum for groups of children and for individual children should be based on knowledge of child development and on careful observation of children at play.

4. Children's language skills are the best predictors of academic success. Development of children's English language skills should be a major goal of the preschool curriculum. Early childhood is a critical time in the development of vocabulary and other language skills. These skills provide the foundation for learning to read and write and for later academic achievement.

5. Developmental domains are highly interrelated. Development in one domain influences the development in other domains. This interrelationship must be considered in planning preschool programs. For example, children's mathematical learning may occur on the playground, in dramatic play, and while using sensory materials.

6. Young children learn by doing. Teachers should provide opportunities for children to explore materials, to engage in physical activities, and to interact with peers and adults. A balance of child-initiated and teacher-selected activities will maximize children's learning.

7. Families are the primary caregivers and educators of their young children. Program staff must give families the information they may need to support their children's learning and development. Program staff and families should also work together to ensure that children are provided with the best learning experiences possible at home and at preschool.

Guidelines for Preschool Learning Experiences structures learning through play and meaningful activities in a developmental sequence. The mark of a superior teacher is the ability to select materials and interact with children in ways that help them learn through their own play and these planned activities. Young children need many and varied opportunities to:

- **Plan:** children consider what they are going to do with materials and how they are going to do it.
- **Play:** children use materials and equipment in ways that best suit their personal curiosity and understanding.
- **Reflect:** children recall things that happened to them, reinforcing or questioning their understandings.
- **Revisit:** children practice skills and replay experiences in many different ways, with each activity refining or modifying previous learning.
- **Connect:** children, with the help of staff, connect new knowledge with past experiences, creating links among subject areas and areas of skill development.

III *Massachusetts Arts Curriculum Framework* (November 1999)

DANCE STRANDS AND STANDARDS

STRAND: The Arts Disciplines
Students learn about and use the symbolic language of dance

- **STANDARD 1 - Movement Elements and Dance Skills:**
  Students will identify and demonstrate movement elements and dance skills.

- **STANDARD 3 - Dance as Expression**
  Students will demonstrate an understanding of dance as a way to express and communicate meaning.

- **STANDARD 4 - Performance in Dance**
  Students will rehearse and stage dance works.

- **STANDARD 5 - Critical Response**
  Students will describe and analyze their own dances and the dances of others using appropriate dance vocabulary. When appropriate, students will connect their analysis to interpretation and evaluation.

- **STANDARD 10 - Interdisciplinary Connections**
  Students will apply their knowledge of the arts to the study of English language arts, foreign languages, health, history and social science, mathematics, and science and technology/engineering.

MUSIC STRANDS AND STANDARDS

STRAND: The Arts Disciplines
Students learn about and use the symbolic language of music

- **STANDARD 1 - Singing**
  Students will sing, alone and with others, a varied repertoire of music.

- **STANDARD 2 - Reading and Notation**
  Students will read music written in standard notation.

- **STANDARD 3 - Playing Instruments**
  Students will play instruments, alone and with others, to perform a varied repertoire of music.

- **STANDARD 4 - Improvisation and Composition**
  Students will improvise, compose, and arrange music.

- **STANDARD 5 – Critical Response**
  Students will describe and analyze their own music and the music of others using appropriate music vocabulary. When appropriate, students will connect their analysis to interpretation and evaluation

STRAND: Connections: History, Criticism, and Links to Other Disciplines
Students learn about the history and criticism of music, its role in the community, and its links to other disciplines

- **STANDARD 6 - Purposes and Meanings in the Arts**
  Students will describe the purposes for which works of dance, music, theatre, visual arts, and architecture were and are created, and, when appropriate, interpret their meanings.

- **STANDARD 10 - Interdisciplinary Connections**
  Students will apply their knowledge of the arts to the study of English language arts, foreign languages, health, history and social science, mathematics, and science and technology/engineering.

THEATER ARTS STRANDS AND STANDARDS

STRAND: The Arts Disciplines
Students learn about and use the symbolic languages of theatre

- **STANDARD 1 - Acting**
  Students will develop acting skills to portray characters who interact in improvised and scripted scenes.

- **STANDARD 3 - Directing**
  Students will rehearse and stage dramatic works.

- **STANDARD 4 - Technical Theatre**
  Students will demonstrate skills in using the basic tools, media, and techniques involved in theatrical production.

- **STANDARD 5 - Critical Response**
  Students will describe and analyze their own theatrical work and the work of others using appropriate theatre vocabulary. When appropriate, students will connect their analysis to interpretation and evaluation.

STRAND: Connections: History, Criticism, and Links to Other Disciplines
Students learn about the history and criticism of theater, its role in the community, and its links to other disciplines

- **STANDARD 10 - Interdisciplinary Connections**
  Students will apply their knowledge of the arts to the study of English language arts, foreign languages, health, history and social science, mathematics, and science and technology/engineering.

VISUAL ARTS STRANDS AND STANDARDS

STRAND: The Arts Disciplines
Students learn about and use the symbolic language of the visual arts

- **STANDARD 1 – Methods, Materials, and Techniques**
  Students will demonstrate knowledge of the methods, materials, and techniques unique to the visual arts.
  - Students will use a variety of media, for example, crayons, chalk, paint, clay, various kinds of paper, textiles, and yarns, and understand how to use them to produce different visual effects

- Students will create artwork in a variety of two-dimensional and three-dimensional media
- Learn to use appropriate vocabulary related to methods, materials, and techniques
- Learn to take care of materials and tools and use them safely

- **STANDARD 2 – Elements and Principals of Design**
  Students will demonstrate knowledge of the elements and principals of design
  - color (primary, secondary)
  - line (explore a wide variety of types of lines in environment and in artwork)
  - texture (use in 2D and 3D artworks and in the environment)
  - shape and form (identify simple shapes and their use in art and in the environment—circles, squares, spheres, cones cubes
  - pattern (in artwork and in the environment)

- **STANDARD 3 – Observation, Abstraction, Invention, and Expression**
  Students will demonstrate their powers of observation, abstraction, invention, and expression in a variety of media, materials, and techniques

- **STANDARD 4 – Drafting, Revising, and Exhibiting**
  Students will demonstrate knowledge of the processes of creating and exhibiting their own artwork: drafts, critique, self-assessments, refinement, and exhibit preparation

- **STANDARD 5 – Critical Response**
  Students will describe and analyze their own work and the work of others using appropriate visual arts vocabulary. When appropriate, students will connect their analysis to interpretation and evaluation

- **Interdisciplinary Connections**
  Students will apply their knowledge of the arts to the study of English language arts, foreign languages, health, history and social science, mathematics, and science and technology/engineering.

IV *Massachusetts Curriculum Framework for English Language Arts and Literacy, Incorporating the Common Core State Standards for English Language Arts and Literacy in History/Social Studies, Science, and Technical Subjects* (March 2011)

Reading Standards for Literature (Pre-K):

Key Ideas and Details
- MA.1. With prompting and support, ask and answer questions about a story or poem read aloud.
- MA.2. With prompting and support, retell a sequence of events from a story read aloud.
- MA.3. With prompting and support, act out characters and events from a story or poem read aloud.

Craft and Structure
- MA.8.A. Respond with movement or clapping to a regular beat in poetry or song.
- MA.10. Listen actively as an individual and as a member of a group to a variety of age-appropriate literature read aloud
- MA.4. With prompting and support, ask and answer questions about unfamiliar words in a story or poem read aloud.
- MA.5. Recognize common types of texts (e.g. storybooks, poems)
- MA.6. With prompting and support, "read" the illustrations in a picture book by describing a character or place depicted, or by telling how a sequence of events unfolds

Integration of Knowledge and Ideas
- MA.7. With prompting and support, make predictions about what happens next in a picture book after examining and discussing illustrations
- MA.8.A. Respond with movement or clapping to a regular beat in poetry or song
- MA.9. With prompting and support, make connections between a story or poem and one's own experiences

Range of Reading and Level of Complexity
- MA.10. Listen actively as an individual and as a member of a group to a variety of age-appropriate literature read aloud

Reading Standards: Foundational Skills (Pre-K):

Print Concepts
- ☐ MA.1. With guidance and support, demonstrate understanding of the organization and basic features of printed and written text: books, words, letters, and the alphabet
- ☐ MA.1.a. Handle books respectfully and appropriately, holding them right side up and turning pages one at a time from front to back
- ☐ MA.1.d. Recognize and name some uppercase letters of the alphabet and the lowercase letters in one's own name

Phonological Awareness
- ☐ MA.2. With guidance and support, demonstrate understanding of spoken words, syllables, and sounds
- ☐ MA.2.a. With guidance and support, recognize and produce rhyming words
- ☐ MA.2.c. With guidance and support, identify the initial sound of a spoken word and, with guidance and support, generate several other words that have the same initial sound

Phonics and Word Recognition
- ☐ MA.3. Demonstrate beginning understanding of phonics and word analysis skills
- ☐ MA.3.a. Link an initial sound to a picture of an object that begins with that sound and, with guidance and support, to the corresponding printed letter
- ☐ MA.3.c. Recognize one's own name and familiar common signs and labels (e.g. STOP)

Writing Standards (Pre-K):

Text Types and Purposes
- ☐ MA.1. Dictate words to express a preference or opinion about a topic
- ☐ MA.2. Use a combination of dictating and drawing to explain information about a topic
- ☐ MA.3. Use a combination of dictating and drawing to tell a real or imagined story

Production and Distribution of Writing
- ☐ MA.6. Recognize that digital tools (e.g. computers, cell phones, cameras, and other devices,) are used for communication and, with support and guidance, use them to convey messages in pictures and/or in words

Speaking and Listening Standards (Pre-K):

Comprehension and Collaboration
- MA.1. Participate in collaborative conversations with diverse partners during daily routines and play
- MA.1.a Observe and use appropriate ways of interacting in a group, (e.g. taking turns in talking, listening to peers, waiting to speak until another person is finished talking, asking questions and waiting for an answer, gaining the floor in appropriate ways)
- MA.2. Recall information for short periods of time and retell, act out, or represent information from text read aloud, a recording, or a video (e.g. watch a video about birds and their habitats and make drawings or constructions of birds and their nests)
- MA.3. Ask and answer questions in order to seek help, get information, or clarify something that is not understood

Presentation of Knowledge and Ideas
- MA.4. Describe personal experiences; tell real or imagined stories
- MA.5. Create representations of experiences or stories (e.g. drawings, constructions with blocks or other materials, clay models) and explain them to others
- MA.6. Speak audibly and express thoughts, feelings, and ideas

Language Standards (Pre-K):

Conventions of Standard English
- MA.1. Demonstrate use of oral language in informal, everyday settings

Vocabulary Acquisition and Use
- MA.4. Ask and answer questions about the meanings of new words and phrases introduced through books, activities, and play
- MA.5.a. Demonstrate understanding of concepts by sorting common objects into categories (e.g. sort objects by color, shape, or texture)
- MA.6. Use words and phrases acquired through conversations, listening to books read aloud, activities, and play

V	*Massachusetts Curriculum Framework for Mathematics, Incorporating the Common Core State Standards for Mathematics* **(March 2011)**

Content Standards (Pre-K):

Know Number Names and Counting Sequence
- MA.1. Listen to and say the names of numbers in meaningful contexts
- MA.2. Recognize and name written numerals 0-10

Count to Tell the Number of Objects
- MA.3. Understand the relationships between numerals and quantities up to ten

Compare Numbers
- MA.4. Count many kinds of concrete objects and actions up to ten, using one-to-one correspondence, and accurately count as many as seven things in a scattered configuration

Operations and Algebraic Thinking
- Understand addition as putting together and adding to, and understand subtraction as taking apart and taking from

Measurement and Data
- Classify objects and count the number of objects in each category
- Work with money

Geometry
- Identify and describe shapes (squares, circles, triangles, rectangles)

VI	*Massachusetts Science and Technology/Engineering Curriculum Framework* **(October 2006)**

Earth and Space Science
- Recognize that water, rocks, soil, and living organisms are found on the earth's surface
- Understand that air is a mixture of gases that is all around us and that wind is moving air
- Describe the weather changes from day to day and over the seasons
- Recognize that the sun supplies heat and light to the earth and is necessary for life

- Identify some events around us that have repeating patterns, including the seasons of the year, day and night

Life Science
- Recognize that animals (including humans) and plants are living things that grow, reproduce, and need food, air, and water
- Differentiate between living and nonliving things. Group both living and nonliving things according to the characteristics that they share
- Recognize that plants and animals have life cycles, and that life cycles vary for different living things
- Describe ways in which many plants and animals closely resemble their parents in observed appearance
- Recognize that fossils provide us with information about living things that inhabited the earth years ago
- Recognize that people and other animals interact with the environment through their senses of sight, hearing, touch, smell, and taste
- Recognize changes in appearance that animals and plants go through as the seasons change
- Identify the ways in which an organism's habitat provides for its basic needs (plants require air, water, nutrients, and light; animals require food, water, air, and shelter)

Physical Sciences
- Sort objects by observable properties such as size, shape, color, weight, texture
- Identify objects and materials as solid, liquid, or gas. Recognize that solids have a definite shape and that liquids and gases take the shape of their container
- Describe the various ways that objects can move, such as in a straight line, zigzag, back-and-forth, fast, and slow
- Demonstrate that the way to change the motion of an object is to apply a force (give it a push or a pull). The greater the force, the greater the change in the motion of the object
- Recognize that under some conditions, objects can be balanced

Technology and Engineering
1. Materials and Tools
    1.1 Identify and describe characteristics of natural materials (e.g. wood, cotton, fur, wool) and human-made materials (e.g. plastic, Styrofoam)

1.2 Identify and explain some possible uses for natural materials (e.g. wood, cotton, fur, wool) and human-made materials (e.g. plastic, Styrofoam)

1.3 Identify and describe the safe and proper use of tools and materials (e.g. glue, scissors, tape, ruler, paper, toothpicks, straws, spools,) to construct simple structures

2. Engineering Design

2.1 Identify tools and simple machines used for specific purposes (e.g. ramp, wheel, pulley, lever)

2.2 Describe how human beings use parts of the body as tools (e.g. teeth for cutting, hands for grasping and catching) and compare their use with the ways in which animals use those parts of their bodies

VII *Massachusetts History and Social Science Curriculum Framework* (August 2003)

Learning Standards

With guidance from the teacher, students should be able to:

- Identify and describe the events or people celebrated during United States national holidays and why we celebrate them.

    A. Columbus Day
    B. Independence Day
    C. Martin Luther King, Jr. Day
    D. Presidents' Day
    E. Thanksgiving

- Put events in their own and their families' lives in temporal order
- Identify the student's street address, city or town, and Massachusetts as the state and the United States as the country in which he or she lives. Identify the name of the student's school and the city or town in which it is located
- Describe the location and features of places in the immediate neighborhood of the students' home of school
- Retell stories that illustrate honesty, courage, friendship, respect, responsibility, and the wise or judicious exercise of authority, and explain how the characters in the stories show these qualities
- Identify and describe family or community members who promote the welfare and safety of children and adults
- Demonstrate understanding that there are important American symbols by identifying:

   A. the American flag
   B. the melody of the national anthem
   C. the picture and name of the current president
   D. the words of the Pledge of Allegience
- Give examples of different kinds of jobs that people do, including the work they do at home
- Explain why people work (e.g. to earn money in order to buy things they want)
- Give examples of the things that people buy with the money they earn

Concepts and Skills – History and Geography

1. Identify sequential actions such as first, next, last, in stories and use them to describe personal experiences

2. Use correctly words and phrases related to chronology and time (e.g. now, long ago, before, after, morning, afternoon, night, today, tomorrow, yesterday, last or next week, month, year, and past, present future tenses of verbs)

3. Use correctly the word because in the context of stories or personal experiences

4. Use correctly words and phrases that indicate location and direction (e.g. up, down, near, far, left, right, straight, back, behind, in front of)

5. Tell or show what a map is and what a globe is

Concept Skills – Civics and Government

6. Give examples that show the meaning of the following concepts: authority, fairness, justice, responsibility, and rules

Concept Skills – Economics

7. Use words relating to work such as jobs, money, buying, and selling

8. Give examples of how family members, friends, or acquaintances use money directly or indirectly (e.g. credit/debit card, check, cash) to buy things they want

VIII *Massachusetts Comprehensive Health Curriculum Framework* (October 1999)

Physical Health Strand:

Standard 1: Growth and Development
1.1   Name the external and internal parts of the body and the body systems (nervous, muscular, skeletal, circulatory, respiratory, digestive, endocrine, and excretory systems)
1.3   Identify appropriate accommodations and aids for people with physical disabilities

Standard 2: Physical Activity and Fitness
2.1   Apply movement concepts including direction, balance, level (high, low), pathway (straight, curve, zigzag), range (expansive, narrow), and force absorption (rigid, with bent knees) to extend versatility and improve physical performance
2.2   Use a variety of manipulative (throwing, catching, striking), locomotor (walking, running, skipping, hopping, galloping, sliding, jumping, leaping) and non-locomotor (twisting, balancing, extending) skills as individuals and in teams
2.5   Explain the benefits of physical fitness to good health and increased active lifestyle

Standard 3: Nutrition
3.1   Identify the key nutrients in food that support healthy body systems (skeletal, circulatory) and recognize that the amount of food needed changes as the body grows
3.3   Recognize hunger and satiety cues and how to make food decisions based upon these cues
3.6   Describe personal hygiene and safety measures used in preparing foods

Social and Emotional Health Strand:

Standard 5: Mental Health
5.1   Identify the various feelings that most people experience and describe the physical and emotional reactions of the body to intense positive and negative feelings
5.2   Apply methods to accommodate a variety of feelings in a constructive manner in order to promote well-being
5.3   Define character traits such as honesty, trustworthiness, self-discipline, respectfulness, and kindness and describe their contribution to identity, self-concept, decision-making, and interpersonal relationships

Standard 6: Family Life
6.1   Describe different types of families, addressing membership and social influences, and the functions of family members
6.3   Identify whom to talk with about family problems and successes
6.4   Identify what parents do to provide a safe, healthy environment for their children

Safety and Prevention Strand:

Standard 8: Disease Prevention and Control
8.1   Describe how the body fights germs and disease naturally and with medicines and immunization
8.2   Identify the common symptoms of illness and recognize that being responsible for individual health means alerting caretakers to any symptoms of illness
8.3   Apply skills to prevent and control the spread of disease, including those that help promote cleanliness (such as correct handwashing, regular bathing, and washing clothes)
8.4   Identify tooth functions and causes of tooth health and tooth decay, and proper dental health skills (such as choosing healthy snacks, brushing, flossing)

Standard 9: Safety and Injury Prevention
9.1   List rules for fire safety, weapons safety, bus safety, and seatbelt [carseat] use where applicable, such as at home, school, community, and play, and explain why the rules are important
9.2   Name persons and community helpers (such as police officers, fire fighters, and emergency medical personnel) who can be contacted to help with health, safety, and injury prevention and describe the appropriate procedures for contacting healthcare personnel in an emergency

Standard 10: Tobacco, Alcohol, and Substance Use/Abuse Prevention
10.1   Identify and distinguish between substances that are safe and unsafe to be taken by mouth

Standard 11: Violence Prevention
11.1   Describe some of the ways that young children can be intentionally helpful and intentionally hurtful to one another
11.9   Demonstrate effective communication, negotiation, and conflict resolution for resolving potentially violent conflicts

Personal and Community Health Strand:
13.2   Working with family volunteers, students clean up school grounds and plant flowers and other plants that help clean the air (such as spider plants or peace lily). Take before and after pictures and display

BIBLIOGRAPHY

Bibliography

Ariza, E. N., Noorchaya, Y., Zainuddin, H., & Jones, C. A. (2006). *Why TESOL?: theories and issues in teaching English to speakers of other languages in K-12 classrooms* (3rd ed.). Dubuque, Iowa: Kendall/Hunt Pub. Print.

Ashby, M., & Maidment, J. A. (2005). *Introducing Phonetic Science*. Cambridge: Cambridge University Press. Print.

Brooks, M.G. &, B. J. (1999). The Courage to be Constructivist. *Educational Leadership, 57* (n3), 18-24. Print.

Brown, H. D. (2001). *Teaching by Principles: An Interactive Approach to Language Pedagogy* (2nd ed.). White Plains, NY: Longman. Print.

Carlson, N. R. (1977). *Physiology of Behavior*. Boston: Allyn and Bacon. Print.

Colorado Department of Education, "Results Matter Video Series on Early Childhood Assessment." http://www.cde.state.co.us/resultsmatter/RMVideoSeries.htm. Video.

Cook, G. (2003). *Applied Linguistics*. Oxford: Oxford Univ. Press. Print.

Cooper, J. D. (2000). *Literacy: Helping Children Construct Meaning* (4th ed.). Boston: Houghton Mifflin Co. Print.

Crain, W. (2004). *Theories of Development Concepts and Applications.* Boston, Mass: Pearson. Print.

Crosswalk between the 2011 Prekindergarten Standards in English Language Arts and Literacy and the Guidelines for Preschool Learning Experiences. (n.d.). *www.mass.gov/edu/docs/eec/curriculum-and-learning/20110303-crosswalk-english-litercy.pdf*. Retrieved February 18, 2012, from www.mass.gov/edu/docs/eec/curriculum-and-learning/20110303-crosswalk-english-literacy.pdf

Crosswalk between 2011 Prekindergarten Standards in Mathematics and the Guidelines for Preschool Learning Experiences. (n.d.). *-learning/20110303-crosswalk-math.pdf*. Retrieved February 18, 2012, from www.mass.gov/edu/docs/eec/curriculum-and-learning/20110303-crosswalk-math.pdf

Cronin, S., & Masso, C. (2003). *Soy Bilingue: Language, Culture & Young Latino Children*. Seattle, Wash., USA: Center for Linguistic and Cultural Democracy. Print.

Davies, A., & Elder, C. (2004). *The Handbook of Applied Linguistics*. Malden, MA: Blackwell. Print.

DeCapua, A. (2008). *Grammar for Teachers a Guide to American English for Native and Non-native Speakers*. New York: Springer. Print.

Developing early literacy: report of the National Early Literacy Panel : a scientific synthesis of early literacy development and implications of intervention.. (2008). Washington, DC: National Institute for Literacy. Print

Dewey, J. (1897). My Pedagogic Creed. *School Journal, 54*(January 1897), 77-80. Print.

Division for Early Childhood of the Council for Exceptional Children. (2007). "Promoting Positive Outcomes for Children with Disabilities: Recommendations for Curriculum, Assessment, and Program Evaluation." Missoula, MT:Author. Print.

Dockett, S. &, P. B. (2001). Starting School: Effective Transitions. *ECRP Early Childhood Research & Practice, Volume 3 Number 2*(Fall 2001), 1-19. Print.

Dodd, V. J. (2010). *Practical Education Law for the Twenty-first Century* (2nd ed.). Durham, N.C.: Carolina Academic Press. Print.

Echevarria, J., Vogt, M., & Short, D. (2008). *Making Content Comprehensible for English Learners: the SIOP model* (3rd ed.). Boston: Pearson/Allyn and Bacon. Print.

Edwards, C. P., Gandini, L., & Forman, G. E. (1993). *The Hundred Languages of Children: the Reggio Emilia Approach to Early Childhood Education*. Norwood, N.J.: Ablex Pub. Corp. Print.

Eisner, E. S. (2001). What Does it mean to say that a School is doing Well?. *Phi Delta Kappan, 82 n5*(Jan 2001), 367-372. Print.

Freeman, Y. & Freeman, D. Academic Language for English Language Learners and Struggling Readers: How to Help Students Succeed Across Content Areas. Portsmouth NH: Heinemann. 2008. Print.

Freeman, D. E., & Freeman, Y. S. (2004). *Essential Linguistics: What you need to know to Teach Reading, ESL, Spelling, Phonics, and Grammar*. Portsmouth, NH: Heinemann. Print.

Frost, J. L. (2007). The Changing Culture of Childhood: A Perfect Storm. *Childhood Education, 83 n4*(Sum 2007), 225. Print.

Gardner, Howard. "Multiple Lenses on The Mind." ExpoGestion Conference. ExpoGestion. ExpoGestion, Bogota, Colombia. 25 May 2005. Reading. Print.

Hurwitz N. &, H. S. (2000). Do High Stakes Assessments Improve Learning?. *American School Board Journal, Issue 9*(January 2000), 150-160. Print.

James, B. (1989). *Treating Traumatized Children: New Insights and Creative Interventions*. Lexington, Mass.: Lexington Books. Print.

Jung, C. G. (19711966). *The Spirit in Man, Art, and Literature*. Princeton, N.J.: Princeton University Press. Print.

Kagan, J. (1998). "How We Become Who We Are." Family Therapy Networker, n/a (Sept/Oct), 52, 54-63. Print.

Lightbown, P., & Spada, N. M. (2006). *How Languages are Learned* (3rd ed.). Oxford: Oxford University Press. Print.

Little, C., Kagan, S. L., & Frelow, V. S. (2003). *Standards for Preschool Children's Learning and Development: Who has standards, How were they Developed, and How are they Used?*. Greensboro, NC: SERVE. Print.

Massachusetts Department of Early Education and Care 606 CMR 7.00 (2010) "Standards for the Licensure or Approval of Family Child Care; Small Group and School Age and Large Group and School Age Child Care Programs." Print.

Massachusetts Department of Elementary and Secondary Education (November 1999). *Massachusetts Arts Curriculum Framework*. Malden, MA. Print.

Massachusetts Department of Elementary and Secondary Education (October 1999) *Massachusetts Comprehensive Health Curriculum Framework*. Malden, MA. Print

Massachusetts Department of Elementary and Secondary Education (March 2011) *Massachusetts Curriculum Framework for English Language Arts and Literacy, Grades Pre-Kindergarten to 12, Incorporating the Common Core State Standards for Literacy in History/Social Studies, Science, and Technical Subjects*. Malden, MA. Print.

Massachusetts Department of Elementary and Secondary Education (March 2011) *Massachusetts Curriculum Framework for Mathematics, Grades Pre-Kindergarten to 12, Incorporating the Common Core State Standards for Mathematics*. Malden, MA. Print.

Massachusetts Department of Elementary and Secondary Education (August 2003) *Massachusetts History and Social Science Curriculum Framework*. Malden, MA. Print.

Massachusetts Department of Elementary and Secondary Education (October 2006) *Massachusetts Science and Technology/Engineering Curriculum Framework*. Malden, MA. Print

Massachusetts Department of Education (2003). *Early Childhood Program Standards for Three and Four Year Olds.* Malden, MA: Author. Print.

Massachusetts Department of Elementary and Secondary Education, (2003). *Guidelines for Preschool Learning Experiences*. Malden, MA: Author. Print.

Massachusetts Department of Elementary and Secondary Education, (2008). *Kindergarten Learning Experiences*. Malden, MA: Author. Print.

Massachusetts QRIS Standards - Executive Office of Education - Mass.Gov. (n.d.). *Mass.Gov*. Retrieved May 30, 2012, from http://www.mass.gov/edu/birth-grade-12/early-education-and-care/qris/massachusetts-qris-standards.html

McCarthy, M. (2001). *Issues in Applied Linguistics*. Cambridge: Cambridge University Press. Print.

McLaren, P. (1989). Chapter 4 The Emergence of Critical Pedagogy. *Life in schools: an introduction to critical pedagogy in the foundations of education* (pp. 185-192). New York: Longman. Print.

McLaughlin, B. (1992). "Myths and misconceptions about second language learning: What every teacher needs to unlearn." (Educational Practice Report No. 5). Santa Cruz, CA and Washington, DC: National Center for Research on Cultural Diversity and Second Language Learning. Print.

Meyer, C. F. (2009). *Introducing English Linguistics.* Cambridge: Cambridge University Press. Print.

Murcia, M., & Olshtain, E. (2000). *Discourse and Context in Language Teaching: a Guide for Language Teachers.* Cambridge, UK: Cambridge University Press. Print.

Murray, B. (2000). "From Brain Scan to Lesson Plan." APA Monitor, n/a (March), 22-27. Rose, D. H., & Meyer, A. (2002). Teaching Every Student in the Digital Age: Universal Design for Learning. New York: Association for Supervision and Curriculum Development. Print.

NAEYC All Criteria Document. (01/10/2012). Washington, D.C.: NAEYC. Print.

NAEYC Early Learning Standards Creating Conditions for Success. (2002). Washington, D.C.: NAEYC. Print.

NAEYC position statement: Early Childhood Curriculum, Assessment, and Program Evaluation. (2003). Washington, D.C.: NAEYC. Print.

NAEYC position statement: Early Childhood Mathematics Promoting Good Beginnings. (adopted in 2002, updated in 2010). Washington, D.C.: NAEYC. Print.

NAEYC position statement: Learning to Read and Write Developing Appropriate Practices for Young Children. (May 1998). Washington, D.C.: NAEYC. Print.

NAEYC position statement: Responding to Linguistic and Cultural Diversity Recommendations for Effective Early Childhood Education. (November 1995). Washington, D.C.: NAEYC. Print.

The NICHD study of early child care and youth development findings for children up to age 4 1/2 years.. (2006). Rockville, Md.: U.S. Dept. of Health and Human Services, National Institutes of Health, National Institute of Child Health and Human Development. Print.

Peregoy, S. F., Boyle, O., & Kaplan, K. (2008). *Reading, Writing and Learning in ESL: a Resource Book for Teaching K-12 English Learners* (5th ed., New ed.). Boston: Pearson. Print.

Power, B.M. & Hubbard, R.S. Language Development: A Reader for Teachers. Columbus, OH: Merrill. 2002. Print.

Promoting Positive Outcomes for Children with Disabilities: Recommendations for Curriculum, Assessment, and Program Evaluation. (0). Washington, D.C.: National Association for the Education of Young Children. Print.

QRIS - Executive Office of Education - Mass.Gov. (n.d.). *Mass.Gov.* Retrieved May 30, 2012, from http://www.mass.gov/edu/birth-grade-12/early-education-and-care/qris/

Report of the National Reading Panel: teaching children to read : an evidence-based assessment of the scientific research literature on reading and its implications for reading instruction.. (2000). Washington, D.C.: National Institute of Child Health and Human Development, National Institutes of Health. Print.

Rose, D. H., & Meyer, A. (2002). Teaching Every Student in the Digital Age: Universal Design for Learning. New York: Association for Supervision and Curriculum Development. Print.

Sen John Kerry's Advisory Committee on Child Care & Small Business. *The Business of Childcare.* Massachusetts. Print.

Smith, P. H. (2011). *Mapping Applied Linguistics.* London: Routledge. Print.

Tuan, Y. (1977). *Space and Place: the Perspective of Experience.* Minneapolis: University of Minnesota Press. Print.

Wright, P. W., & Wright, P. D. (2007). *Wrightslaw: Special Education Law* (2nd ed.). Hartfield, Va.: Harbor House Law Press. Print.

Zumthor, P. (2010). *Thinking Architecture.* Basel: Birkhauser. Print.

About the Author

Roselle P. O'Brien is a licensed educator and licensed School Adjustment Counselor. She holds a Master of Arts Degree in Education in Language Arts, Literacy, and Curriculum Design, a Master of Fine Arts Degree in Creative Writing, and a Master of Arts Degree in Clinical Mental Health Counseling. She is a Licensed Mental Health Counselor and a licensed nurse. Roselle lives in Boston.

www.ingramcontent.com/pod-product-compliance
Lightning Source LLC
Chambersburg PA
CBHW082141230426
43672CB00016B/2933